TIMES
of the
YEAR

Filled with the Glory of God

Bishop Everett H Jefferson, Sr.

Angela M. Sinkfield-Gray
Editor

WESTBOW PRESS®
A DIVISION OF THOMAS NELSON & ZONDERVAN

WestBow Press books may be ordered through booksellers or by contacting:

WestBow Press
A Division of Thomas Nelson & Zondervan
1663 Liberty Drive
Bloomington, IN 47403
www.westbowpress.com
844-714-3454

ISBN: 978-1-6642-6643-8 (sc)
ISBN: 978-1-6642-6642-1 (e)

Print information available on the last page.

WestBow Press rev. date: 06/09/2022

CONTENTS

DEDICATION

I dedicate this book to my wife, three sons, and two daughters, Everett Jefferson Jr., Eric Jefferson, and Elliot Jefferson; Dorsharica Jefferson and Schnelle Jefferson and my ministerial colleagues. My sons and daughter have given me an abundance of ministerial support by the preaching and teaching of the Gospel, administrative, and musical help for the building of the kingdom of God. I thank my wife, Elaine W. Jefferson for her committed effort in helping me with the promotion and sales of this book and others helps that allow me to continue working on the charge the Lord has given me. My wife has given me her constant encouragement to express my God given thoughts through public speaking, writing, and publishing. Her God given motivation inspires me to keep writing even in my sickness and pain. I love Elaine and pray she will be with me throughout the time Almighty God gives us both on earth. I also dedicate this book to the memories of my mother, the late Katie Jefferson, and grandmother, the late Pearl Juitt, schoolteachers who encouraged me to learn the necessary course work for my career in public speaking and writing. My father the late Percy Jefferson who encouraged me to do well in school and live according to the Laws of God. Other schoolteachers through my educational career allowed me to be proficient at educational studies, practice English, Language Arts, and other academic studies that would help me be efficient in my educational career. My educators also taught me to be efficient in communication skills that allowed me to be successfully with my peers. I am grateful for the late Dr. Steven Haymon Ed. D, a professor of psychology who has written several books in his field and practiced psychology in the greater Saint Louis, Missouri area. The Professors of the Loyola University of Maryland provided me with the necessary skills to write and helped me to develop the art of expression through writing. My biblical skills and knowledge were developed at the Bethesda Temple Church in St. Louis, Missouri, pastored by the late Bishop James A. Johnson. It is difficult to name all the people that had a great influence in my life. Many relatives, schoolteachers, friends, and co-workers have encouraged me to do great things and helped me to continue in my educational field. I have learned so much from so many people. I love and respect those who helped me achieve the wisdom and knowledge to express myself verbally and literally. I am grateful to acknowledge all that have given me wisdom to express God's word and live in a domain that gives courage and strength to live what I teach and preach. I believe that expressing the good things in life and encouraging others to be good citizens of heaven is part of our commitment on earth. We should also be helpful to others growing and developing in the good things that Almighty God desires for all of us to do. I will always be grateful for the help I have received throughout my spiritual and educational career. I pray God's richest blessing upon all that have helped me to become the husband, minister, teacher, and friend that I am today.

PREFACE

The born-again believer has many challenges in and out of church that often conflict and try to eradicate what we believe. Many conflicts come through our association with nonbelievers in our life, and things that are negatively spoken on our jobs, neighborhoods, and through social media. We are easily persuaded by the motivation of the majority of people and especially our peers. The introduction of multimedia has made a great influence, especially on the younger generation. I am confident that what we are witnessing today will increase and influence many to be challenged by participating in every new concept that is introduced. Many of these new concepts are educational and will increase learning in our educational system. I do not criticize the introduction of new technology and educational devices. However, I am concerned about the use of technology and devices that introduce negative behavior in the hearts of many. I have come to the conclusion that the word of God Almighty is correct and there is nothing that can separate us from the love of God. It does not matter how the world changes and what things are created as evil and ungodly devices used to introduce ungodly concepts. Nevertheless, as these things are created, Almighty God will give us the wisdom to change the evil into good as we vigorously fight the enemy and win. Ungodly concepts are being introduced constantly each day. Many people are accepting these concepts and allowing them to destroy their lives. Isn't this what is happening to many people? We were lost in sin and the Lord found us and saved us. Many people who practiced evil things are now saved and walking in Christ Jesus. This is the miraculous work of Almighty God! We were once blind but now we see, lost but now we are found. There has been given a great change in our lives, and Almighty God is desiring us to be productive in the kingdom of God. This book uses an agriculture metaphor to explain the spiritual concepts in the Bible. I use the agriculture concepts because it was a major part of my life growing up in the southern states of Arkansas and Missouri. I found it interesting that the use of agricultural concepts was often used in the Bible. It is my desire to use these concepts expressed to explain biblical principles. The actions of each month are related to scriptural text that will help individuals understand and make the word of Almighty God relevant to our everyday life. Each month has it's biblical and everyday natural examples showing us how to understand biblical principles through the life and times we live naturally. After studying the Bible, I find that Jesus gave many natural concepts explaining spiritual things (parables). When parables are used, it helps us to understand the spiritual meaning through natural concepts. I will use each month and its most celebrated time to help the reader understand natural and spiritual concepts in unison with spiritual things and their application in our lives. When these concepts are applied in our spiritual walk, we will easily understand spiritual things and develop a consecrated walk with Christ Jesus. As we take our time and journey through this text, we will find interesting concepts that will enhance our natural and biblical knowledge that will enrich our lives with great blessings. Let us take a spiritual and natural journey through each month of the year that will enhance our knowledge and love for nature and the word of God.

INTRODUCTION

Living in the South and Midwest I found it fascinating to see all the produce grown and harvested from market to consumption. It was amazing to see things grow from a tiny seed to vegetables and fruit that are appealing to the eyes and satisfying to the taste. It almost seems like a miracle to watch things grow from a tiny seed to a large plant producing an abundance of fruit that was one hundred times larger than the tiny seed. If you have never seen the agricultural process at work, you will be astonished at the way it works and how much produce is gained from a tiny seed. It reminds me of the analogy our Lord Jesus uses when He talks about the power of faith. The scriptures declare: ***"Then He said, "To what shall we liken the kingdom of God? Or with what parable shall we picture it? It is like a mustard seed which, when it is sown on the ground, is smaller than all the seeds on earth; but when it is sown, it grows up and becomes greater than all herbs, and shoots out large branches, so that the birds of the air may nest under its shade." (Mark 4:30-32, NKJV).*** If we understand the parable of the mustard seed, we will understand the mechanics of gardening and how faith works in the heart of the believer. Just like the plants and seeds that I talk about in this book I believe we can use the same analogy to discuss and increase our faith in Christ Jesus. When we plant a seed, we cannot leave it alone for nature to produce the crops we desire. The seeds we plant go through a process called germination (to cause the seed to sprout or develop). When the seed grows it comes through the soil and the soil becomes hardend around the infant plant. The ground is broken up around the plant to give air to enhance growth. Likewise, our faith develops somewhat the same way. We plant a spiritual seed, but we do not leave it to its own to develop and produce fruit. Remember the scripture by the Apostle Paul? ***"I planted, Apollos watered, but God gave the increase." (1 Corinthians 3:6, NKJV).*** It takes work by many to help plants develop to successful vegetables and fruit that will be a blessing to others and ourselves. When seeds are planted weeds will grow up with them. It is necessary that weeds are removed from around the plants, so the desired nutrients are used for the plants and not the weeds. Analogous to the growing of our gardens is the growing of our faith. When we hear the word of the Lord, faith takes root in our spirit. The word we read from the Holy Scriptures and hear from the Voice of God gives us faith to do great thing in the earth. Nevertheless, just as the weeds are removed from around the plants, we remove sin and unrighteous acts from our lives. Have you ever looked at a garden and its plants are covered with weeds? Not a pretty sight to see! People familiar with agriculture realize that the weeds must be removed in order for our desired plants to produce the fruit and vegetables we desire and use. Our Lord Jesus desires righteousness from His children. Almighty God has planted us in His garden of love, joy, and peace. We can walk in the righteousness of the Lord God showing the world that we have been born of the water and spirit and we are children of Almighty God! Have you considered being born-again by the water and spirit? It is the most wonderful advent you will ever experience in your life! Have you ever considered why the Lord Jesus came to earth? He came to earth to save sinners, which we were. We do not have to wait any longer. The Lord Jesus has made it possible through His resurrection, for every person to come unto Him and be saved and enjoy eternal life. Let us see what's instore for us who turn their lives over to our Lord Jesus and enjoy the salvation He gives.

JANUARY

The Power of Prayer First

"Therefore, I say to you, whatever things you ask when you pray, believe that you receive them, and you will have them." (Mark 11:24, NKJV*)***.

The Lord God Almighty uses the faith in us to show all of mankind how great He is, and the power that He places in us that we might continue to believe and be spiritually successful. That little seed of faith in us will show the world how great and magnificent the Lord God is! It is the action of Almighty God in His children that motivates the people in the world to believe and experience the movement and power of the Lord God! Our Heavenly Father loves us and is willing do whatever it takes to please us; and at the same time assures us a place in the kingdom of heaven. However, there are enemies that are against us that will do whatever they can to block the flow of God's blessings in our lives. Unbelief, doubts and fears are our worst enemies. The promises in the Bible are null and void in the presence of unbelief, doubt, and fear. These three words are the greatest enemies to the child of Almighty God. Unbelief, doubt and fear will cause us to miss out on an abundance of blessings that God has in store for us. These three will also keep us from communicating with our

Lord and our brothers and sisters in Christ. This communication will give us faith to believe and experience the glory of God. When we fight against the word that Almighty God has given us, we may become spiritually irritated and give up on the promises that the Lord God is willing to give. Are you aware of this spirit when we get sick, when we are broke, or when facing a situation that could cause us shame? The denial of great blessings in our life starts with unbelief. This unbelief has its beginning with our unwillingness to read the promises that Almighty God has made available to us. Please pay attention to this scripture: ***"Now He did not do many mighty works there because of their unbelief." (Matthew 13:58, NKJV).*** Consider the previous scripture listed. "Unbelief" is a dream killer, a spiritual corrupter, and a self-destructive force to our beliefs and faith. How can we receive anything from the Lord if we do not believe? The word of God inspires and motivates us to overcome our doubts and fears by believing every word that the Lord God has spoken. Faith is a word from Almighty God. When we hear God speak, changes will take place in our situations and we should expect great things from our Savior.

Faith never dies, but it can remain in a potential (stored/inactive) spiritual state, and we will never see the movement of Almighty God working on our behalf. However, if we allow our faith to move to a kinetic (moving/active) state the acts of Almighty God will become unlimited! It is the activation of our faith that destroys the words and works of the enemy. The Lord God understands that fear will immobilize our movement towards success and keep us from getting the promises that lies in wait for us! It is not ceremonial acts that declare us righteous by Almighty God but a declaration of faith and unfailing belief that moves God and places us in a position of favor. But for us to experience great favor from Almighty God we must have at least little faith, fully persuaded that the Lord can do anything, and we must remove doubts and unbelief from our minds. The question I ask you today, are you fully persuaded? Do you know the voice of Almighty God? Are you listening to the Lord and not the voice of unbelieving people and the enemy?

The acts of faith that we have discussed are empowered in us if we allow the word of God to be an important part of our lives. If you are an infant in Christ, your desire is to obtain the sincere milk of the word and grow in grace and in the knowledge of our Savior. When we grow in grace and knowledge of our Savior, we obtain the necessary spiritual muscle to fight the enemy and win! I believe our Heavenly Father wants us to grow spiritually so that when there is a need to fight, we will overcome the enemy and win. We will become a part of that great cloud of witnesses that encourages other born-again believers to rise to the occasion and fight the good fight of faith. We will offer praise to Almighty God for leading us into all truths and revelations of His Word that we might become wise children in the kingdom of God. Many have come to realize that specific wisdom comes from specific people and specific intuitions that the Lord has allowed to be established. If we want to be a doctor we go to medical school and if we wish to become an engineer, we attend a school of engineering, which focuses on the science of engineering or other educational disciplines. If we are to be built up on our most Holy faith, we must enter the school of spiritual arts and sciences taught by our Lord and Savior Jesus Christ. We accomplish this Christian education by attending one or more of the many Christian schools that are designed to help us understand the many aspects of Christian education. When we go to school one of the most important criteria is listening. If we cannot listen, we will fail the course and drop out. I believe that our Lord Jesus does not want any of His children to fail. Almighty God will open our understanding to receive the word, which is planted in our heart and soul to make us spiritually strong to fight the good fight of faith. Each day when we add the word of God to our spiritual lives we grow and see a greater manifestation of the word of God. We will experience the movement of Almighty God in us to give us great faith and the power to overcome the power of the enemy. During the beginning of each year many people will make a list of things they often refer to as resolutions. In their hearts, they resolve to change certain things in their lives to make themselves better. We know the story; many times before the month of January is over the things they resolve to do or not do is ended and they are back to the same old things that they are used to do. Some of these things that they resolved not to do is positive in helping with their health, attitude towards others, or overall mental improvement. When we go back to the old way of life, we are inviting the old nature to stay around which could likely lead to unhappiness, sickness or even death.

Nevertheless, I am convinced I do not need a New Year's resolution for my wellbeing but a commitment to Almighty God and a quest for His help for whatever I need to make me healthy and spiritually strong. Do you remember this scripture? ***"If you abide in Me, and My words abide in you, you will ask what you desire, and it shall be done for you." (John 15:7, NKJV).*** Our simple commitment for change is to sincerely ask Almighty God for whatever we need to improve our lives. How many times have we relied on our own way of making changes and the change we desired failed? Have you considered after trying to change situations in your life and unfortunately you failed? There is a breaking point in each of our lives that comes to the place that advises us to try something else other than same old method that does not bring about change. The power of the Holy Spirit in every born-again believer is enough to make even the most dramatic changes for our lives. If great changes are not taking place in your life consider the scripture ***(John 15:7, NKJV)*** previously quoted. Are you abiding in Christ Jesus, and is the Spirit of the Lord and His Word abiding in you? If we seriously consider these three questions you will make the greatest effort to abide in Christ Jesus and experience great results in your lives.

Each day we live unto the Lord with hope and expectation of the Lord's return to receive His church into the kingdom of heaven.

The beginning of the year, month, or week is a great time to start making changes that will positively affect your life. We will remember these changes and the things that we made to glorify Almighty God. The strength that God Almighty gave us to accomplish these things will bring positive and great accomplishments in our lives. I think that most of us have come to realize that many times positive changes and outcomes are not easy. We live in a world where ungodly forces are constantly bombarding us to make unwise choices that negatively affect our lives. The enemy wants to see us fail and accept the things in life that are negatively leading us to an unproductive life. But if we hold fast to what Almighty God has spoken to us, we will be assured to receive the best things in life. Consider every phase of your life and never leave the Lord out of your plans. Remember the wise council of King Solomon found in:

> ***(Proverbs 3:6-8, NKJV)***
> ***"In all your ways acknowledge Him,***
> ***And He shall direct your paths.***
> ***Do not be wise in your own eyes;***
> ***Fear the Lord and depart from evil."***
> ***It will be health to your flesh,***
> ***And strength to your bones.***

Whenever there are major or minor decisions to be made, I will make my request known to Almighty God. Over my life I have found this biblical truth to be meaningful and productive for my life. The truth of the written and spoken word of Almighty God will give great benefits to our lives and we will not be ashamed of the outcome that we receive. Once we see the movement of Almighty God in our lives we will no longer rely on resolutions, wishing and hoping that the things we desire come true. I have come to realize that to see our desires come true is to pray, believe, and expect the movement of Almighty God to become a living reality. Our Lord Jesus designed prayer in the believers that we may see the glory of Almighty God in our lives and experience His power working through us that others may see and eventually believe. Consider the scripture: ***"Be anxious for nothing, but in everything by prayer and supplication, with thanksgiving, let your requests be made known to God; and the peace of God, which surpasses all understanding, will guard your hearts and minds through Christ Jesus." (Philippians 4:6-7, NKJV).*** Also consider what the scriptures say to us, *"We are witnesses."* The movement of Almighty God in us and through us is a powerful example to the world that the Spirit of the Lord lives in us and is functioning in us the things that the Lord desires to show the world.

When we allow the Spirit of the living God to work in us, we become witnesses for the kingdom of heaven in word and deed. People will see the Spirit of Almighty God working in and through us showing the world that Christ abides in us and is doing great things to motivate people to accept the salvation of our Lord Jesus Christ. Such great works in and through us motivates Christians to continue their God given work and help others to develop and continue their work in Christ Jesus. I have come to realize that prayer is one of the most important if not the most important task of a Christian's life. Just as humans need to communicate with each other, we must communicate with our Heavenly Father and our brothers and sisters in Christ. Our Heavenly Father designed a way for us to communicate with Him and it is called prayer. Through prayer we can express our love, request specific things, and call on the name of the Lord to help us through difficult situations. Aren't you glad you have such a wonderful Savior? As we begin our journey with the month of January, we will be become aware of the things necessary to develop and start a successful garden. The information we share will be necessary to develop great plants through the soil that houses the seeds and plants we will place in the ground. Let's consider these scriptures as a base for continued reading.

(Isaiah 53:1-5, NKJV)

Who has believed our report?
And to whom has the arm of the Lord been revealed?
For He shall grow up before Him as a tender plant,
And as a root out of dry ground.
He has no form or comeliness;
And when we see Him,
There is no beauty that we should desire Him.
He is despised and rejected by men,
A Man of sorrows and acquainted with grief.
And we hid, as it were, our faces from Him;
He was despised, and we did not esteem Him.
Surely, He has borne our griefs
And carried our sorrows;
Yet we esteemed Him stricken,
Smitten by God, and afflicted.
But He was wounded for our transgressions,
He was bruised for our iniquities;
The chastisement for our peace was upon Him,
And by His stripes we are healed.

Our Christian life is completely ingrained in and centered around our Lord Jesus Christ. Jesus' death, burial and resurrection allowed us the opportunity to repent from our sins and give our lives completely over to Christ. We must remember that every soul borne after Adam had sinned was destined to die. Adam and Eve were removed from the Garden of Eden and suffer the pronouncement of death because of Adam's disobedience. Nevertheless, the Lord God loved the man He had made and decided to make a way for human beings to be saved and return back to Almighty God. The Lord God made it that way through our Lord Jesus Christ! We no longer need to suffer from the penalty of sin that Adam brought into the world. Jesus suffered for the sin of the whole world. Man could not deal with the punishment of sin that was on his life. Nevertheless, Christ was the only One that could die for the sins of the whole world and fill us with His Spirit that we would have the right to the tree of life. When we consider this great love, we rejoice with great joy and commit our lives to the One that gave His life for our redemption. Jesus not only made a way for us to be saved, but also gave us the power to overcome the sin in the world. We now have the right to live spiritually and glorify Almighty God for the complete salvation that has come into our lives.

FEBRUARY

The Power of Love

"But God, who is rich in mercy, because of His great love with which He loved us, even when we were dead in trespasses, made us alive together with Christ (by grace you have been saved)" (Ephesians 2:4-5, NKJV).

The words of the Apostle Paul still ring in the hearts of men and women when we read the scriptures today. The words of the Lord spoken by the Apostle Paul give reason to the word of both Testaments to consider what the Lord is saying and our actions before the Lord. For centuries men and women have tried to follow the right things and failed. They have unsuccessfully tried to love others and reverted back to resentment and hatred towards our fellow man. One of the greatest ways of understanding Almighty God is to adhere to the godly attributes that are described in the scriptures. However, the child of God that is studying the scriptures and allowing Almighty God to speak to them is finding out that our connection with the Lord and the fulfillment of the scriptures is not achieved by the works we do, nor the fulfillment of the Mosaic Law, but what we allow the Lord to do in us by His Spirit. What has the Lord placed in us? His Holy Spirit! And what does His Spirit generate in us? Love for Almighty God and love for the people He created. Yes, God has placed His gifts in us, and He expects us to allow His gifts to be used. He also wants us to realize there is something greater than the spiritual gifts, and that's the love of Almighty God working effectively in us. Yes, allow the spiritual gifts to work, and allow the love of God to work even greater! We are not in error when we desire the power and anointed gifts of God. We are not in error when we desire to see Almighty God multiply blessings on people by healing and pronouncing deliverance on others and ourselves. But we miss seeing and admiring the whole picture when the greatest manifestation of all is left out, love! This love comes out of us because the Holy Spirit has created the love of God in us. Remember the words of the Apostle Paul: ***"But earnestly desire the best gifts. And yet I show you a more excellent way." (1 Corinthians 12:31, NKJV).*** That more excellent way is showing the love of God that is given to us through the Holy Spirit.

Paul informs the church that if I have all the spiritual gifts, and I do great things, but do not have love, I am nothing. When Paul says these things, it makes you wonder and rethink your relationship in Christ. It makes you consider why I have been living my spiritual life in the manner that's based on the law and not based on the grace of Almighty God. If we allow God's love to flow uninhibited, we will see the glory of God! I have come to realize, by the Spirit of Almighty God, that the real spiritual things and the glory of God is greater than anything that we can see or imagine on this earth. This is why our Lord Jesus is pushing us into His greatest realm, LOVE! This is why I asked the question...Have You Moved To The Next Level? God never intended for His children to remain in the same spiritual place and under the same conditions the rest of our spiritual lives. Consider this example; Was it the Lord's plan for Israel to remain in the wilderness in captivity? I don't think so. Every time the children of Israel were enslaved by their own sinful ways, Almighty God brought them out. Every time they failed, and repented,

Almighty God restored them back to the blessed state they once achieved. This is an example of God's love for His children and His desire that we move to the next level. Our next level inhabits the greatness of God's love and causes us to share His love with His people and the whole world. Yes, Almighty God wants us to speak prophecy and reveals great revelations. God wants us to lay hands on the sick and allow healing to be achieved. God wants us to speak words of wisdom and knowledge. But the greatest thing Almighty God wants is His children to do is love like He loves! Almighty God wants His children to do great things in His name, but the greatest thing the Lord wants His children to do is to show love to each other and the whole world. Are you willing to receive the gifts and callings that God has ordained for your life, and allow the Spirit of God to work effectively in you, producing the greatest gift, the love of God? There is an old song that expresses the love of God…

The Love of God

The love of God is greater far
Than tongue or pen can ever tell
It goes beyond the highest star
And reaches to the lowest hell
The guilty pair, bowed down with care
God gave His Son to win
His erring child He reconciled
And pardoned from his sin

Could we with ink the ocean fill
And were the skies of parchment made
Were every stalk on earth a quill
And every man a scribe by trade

To write the love of God above
Would drain the ocean dry
Nor could the scroll contain the whole
Though stretched from sky to sky

Hallelujah
Hallelujah
Hallelujah

O love of God, how rich and pure!
How measureless and strong!
It shall forevermore endure
The saints' and angels' song

Consider the word of the Lord: ***"Are all apostles? Are all prophets? Are all teachers? Are all workers of miracles? Do all have gifts of healings? Do all speak with tongues? Do all interpret? But earnestly desire the best gifts. And yet I show you a more excellent way." (1Corinthians 12:29-31, NKJV).*** As children of Almighty God we have desired receiving the fruit if the Spirit and spiritual gifts since the birth of the church. Even the Apostle Paul desired imparting spiritual gifts to the saints and that they all would be filled with the fruit of the spirit as well. It is no doubt that the fruit of the spirit and spiritual gifts would be a great access to the church. However, the Apostle Paul made it very clear that the love of God was the greatest of the spiritual gifts. Note the scripture: ***Though I speak with the tongues of men and of angels, but have not love, I have become sounding brass or a clanging cymbal. And though I have the gift of prophecy, and understand all mysteries and all knowledge, and though I have all faith, so that I could remove mountains, but have not love, I am nothing." (1 Corinthians 13:1-2, NKJV).*** We can have great access to spiritual fruit and gifts, but having the love of Almighty God working in us and moving on the hearts of others is much greater. People will know the love of Almighty God by the love of His children. People cannot see Almighty God but they can witness His love expressed by His children in their words and actions. Our words and actions will cause people to outwardly express the love of God and desire to see more of the love of God in action. Many of us that were drawn to salvation was as a result of God's love working in one of His children that cause an individual to be amazed by the love that flowed from the heart of that person.

Real love will cause a person to think a second time about another person. Real love will cause a person to marvel at the way a person speaks in a loving manner or acts in a way that is gloriously beautiful. Real love is directly from Almighty God. It is not fake, faulty, or trying to take advantage of someone. Real love exemplifies the character of Almighty God. You cannot carry out an act and pretend it to be the character of our Lord Jesus Christ. The things that a real child of God does, are within the will of God and out of the heart of God. The things that are done can be traced back to the word of God (Bible). Just consider the love of Almighty God when He (Jesus Christ) went to Calvary's cross and died for our sins. Note what the word of God declares: ***"For scarcely for a righteous man will one die; yet perhaps for a good man someone would even dare to die. But God demonstrates His own love toward us, in that while we were still sinners, Christ died for us." (Romans 5:7-8, NKJV).*** We were at the worst sinful state we could be, but Christ died for us that we might have access to the tree of life, be forgiven of our sins, and live forever. There was nothing we could have done to gain access to eternal life. Eternal life came through Jesus Christ our Lord! We were filled with the Holy Spirit that we might be justified by faith and have a right to the tree of life. When reading the Holy Scriptures, it is a clear choice that the actions of a born-again believer is the love of Almighty God working in the heart of every believer. My recommendation to every born-again believer is to seek and allow Almighty God to fill you with all His gifts but be sure you are filled with His greatest gift, the gift of LOVE! Remember the declaration by the scriptures? ***"But earnestly desire the best gifts. And yet I show you a more excellent way." (1 Corinthians 12:31, NKJV).*** The Lord desires us to develop and use the best gifts He has to offer. But the more excellent way is allowing the love of God to work effectively in us, that others may witness the love of God working effectively in and through us that it changes the life of the sinner and saint, and the Name of the Lord JESUS is glorified.

MARCH

Determine To Succeed

(Don't Let Go - Nor Quit - No Matter How Hard the Wind Blows)

"And He (the Angel) ***said, let Me go, for the day breaks." But he*** (Jacob) ***said, "I will not let You go unless You bless me!" So He said to him, "What is your name?" He said, "Jacob." And He said, "Your name shall no longer be called Jacob, but Israel; for you have struggled with God and with men, and have prevailed." (Genesis 32:26-28, NKJV).***

You know the end of the story; the Angel blessed Jacob and changed his name to "Israel." The blessing came to him because he was determined to hold on, not let go, and experience the blessings from Almighty God! How determined are we to hold on and see the glory of the Lord happen in our lives? Unfortunately too many people take the path of least resistance and think they are going to receive the greatest reward. Also, when something of great value is presented to us, we shy away because of the great challenge that is required to obtain the promise. We often expect to receive the greatest blessing from the Lord with the least amount of spiritual effort. Nothing in life works that way.

Will we see great movements of Almighty God if we do not communicate with Him? Certainly not! Jacob was determined to experience the blessings of the Lord while wrestling with the Angel and therefore cried out, "I'm not letting go until you bless me!" Think about it, a human being wrestling with an angel, a powerful angelic being, and demanding a blessing from Him! Are you crying with the same intensity, passion, and expectation from Almighty God as Jacob did? Are you determined to hold on to God's Hand of blessings until you receive what He has destined for your life? We all should have Jacob's attitude that we will not let go of the Lord's mighty hand until the glory of the Lord has filled our lives. I'm not letting go of God's love, God's Word of faith, and every fruit of the Spirit because it is the fruit of the Spirit and the Gifts of the Spirit that gives me spiritual life and power! I will also not let go of the word of wisdom, word of knowledge, the spirit of discernment, and other gifts of the Spirit that gives me spiritual insight and power to subdue evil forces on the earth. So I ask you, "Are you determined to succeed spiritually?" We have come to realize that there are so many things that come against us to cause failure. Just like the fierce March winds that roar and howl with a destructive blast on its way destroying most things in its path.

Sometimes as a child my brothers and I had to walk against these winds just to get home from school and work. But we were determined no matter how fierce the winds blew; we were going to make it into the warm comfort of our home. Sometimes it was a great fight against the winds but to make it inside a warm home was worth the fight. Often the winds cut our face so badly we would turn around and walk backwards to avoid the sharp cutting winds from damaging our face. My brothers and I learned all kinds of methods and tricks to keeps us from being hurt by the fierce winds. I learned great natural and spiritual lessons from the battles of the March winds. There are so many things we can learn from the acts of nature. Do you stop to learn from the things that are around us? Or do you consider such things a waste of time and never try to learn from things that are placed before us? None of these things are a waste of time. There is such great knowledge in the things that are placed before us. I believe we can learn from whatever things that are presented to our five senses. However, the greater things we learn are from those things presented to our spiritual senses. We learn so much when we allow the Holy Spirit to teach us and we hold on to the things we have been taught by Almighty God. You will only experience spiritual success if you hold on to the hand of Almighty God and never let go! I am determined to experience all the great things that the Lord God has promised for my life. I am confident that nothing will separate me from the love of God, and whatever the Lord has determined for us to receive we will possess. Are you excited about your future success in Christ? Do not let go or give up on the promises Almighty God has spoken into your life. Believe and live with great expectation! For the scriptures have declared: ***"For all the promises of God in Him are yes, and in Him Amen, to the glory of God through us." (2 Corinthians 1:20, NKJV).***

When we wrestle against the elements of nature or the things of the adversary, there can be a terrible fight that causes headache and spiritual pain. Nevertheless, I believe it's worth the fight to gain an advantage over the enemy. Each time we fight we learn the tactics and moves of the enemy. A good spiritual fighter is not concerned about the human quantity or quality of the fight but the movement of the Lord God in the fight. If the Lord is in the fight, we are sure to win. If we do not win, we learn how to win and the next fight can result in winning for sure! A dedicated child of Almighty God is determined to win the spiritual battles that come their way. This child of the Lord looks for a fight and is determined that winning is a sure thing. Just as we naturally fight against things in the natural, we likewise fight against things in the spirit. In order to win we must be aware of the enemy's devices. The enemy is cunning and crafty and will use his wicked devices to deceive and conquer the children of God. Just like the movements of the March winds. The winds will blow in different directions and at different speeds. We cannot see the movements of these winds but we feel the intensity of its movement's cuttings against our flesh. Likewise, we cannot see the movement of the enemy's adverse actions, but we will see and feel the effects of his devastating blows against our spirit. The enemy is determined to defeat us. Every child of Almighty God will some way experience the attack of the enemy. If you are determined to win you must be determined to fight. Every situation in life teaches that if we are to accomplish great things we must learn how to fight effectively and win. Have you heard the expression? *"Winners don't quit, and quitters don't win!"* There is a great determination in every winner that expresses no quitting in this fight. How can I let go and lose this fight when I am too close to receive the victory? How can I let go when I can taste the victory and I am too close to turn around and give up?

Think about where you are in your walk in Christ. You have fought many battles and by the grace of Almighty God you have won. You may be tired of fighting but you cannot quit now. Victory is just around the corner and you will be celebrating the prize that the Lord Almighty has in store for you. As I said before, *"Quitters never win."* Jacob was determined to win the fight with the Angel! The average person may have given up especially after he was injured by his opponent. Note the scripture: ***"Now when He saw that He did not prevail against him, He touched the socket of his hip; and the socket of Jacob's hip was out of joint as He wrestled with him." (Genesis 32:25, NKJV).*** For the average individual this would be the ideal time to give up when an injury (hip socket out of joint) has occurred. But Jacob was determined, though injured; he wanted to receive the blessing. I believe many born-again Christians have experienced encounters with angels or the enemy and gave up because of the devastating fight and injuries received during the fight. We may have made such expressions as, "It's too difficult, and this is an impossible task," or why is the Lord allowing this to happen to me?" Everything that a child of Almighty God encounters in life is for a specific purpose. Some of the greatest blessings have come from the greatest struggles. I am not willing to give up so easy when the blessings from heaven exceed my expectations! Once the Lord has made me a promise, I will fight with all my might to receive what the Lord has promised. I believe the promises from Almighty God are worth fighting and living for. Remember what the Lord Almighty had in His mind when He shed His Blood on Calvary's cross. We were wretched sinners and certainly worthy of death. But the Lord Jesus went to Calvary's cross and died for every human being. Everyone that accepted His death, burial, and resurrection and was filled with His Spirit and given the promise of eternal life. Our Lord Jesus was determined to overcome the awful cross of Calvary that we may have everlasting life. No human being could have received the punishment our Lord Jesus received. Nevertheless, our Lord died, and rose from the dead that every person may have the right to the tree of life! Our spiritual task will not ever equal the suffering and death that our Lord Jesus Christ went through to save us.

Sometime during our lives we may have experience serious consequences to get to the point we were safe and comfortable in our homes. We may have even escaped the fierce wrath of some competitor to experience safety. However, nothing we went through or going to go through compares to the cross of Calvary that brought all of us so great salvation. I am convinced that our determination to succeed in Christ is fueled by the power of Almighty God and the faith that is given to us by His word. When I see the greatness of the Lord working in the church and through His children, I am convinced to remain steadfast in Christ and see the glory of the Lord in the earth. I am determined since I obtained salvation in nineteen seventy-one; to hold on to God's unchaining Hand and continue to experience the mighty acts in the earth. I cannot let go of the Hand of Almighty God. I cannot live spiritually or naturally without the mind of Christ Jesus working in me. I have found Jesus to be my best friend and the lover of my soul. After these many years in Christ I have experience the fierce winds blowing and some hard times trying to make me give up. There were times that people turned against me and I was left all alone. There were times I even felt like giving up and walking away from my salvation. But in these times, I heard the voice of our Lord Jesus Christ telling me not to quit but look ahead, relying on every word that the Lord Jesus has spoken. It was necessary to receive the word in faith believing that victory will be done! The key words to our success in New Testament Christian living are obedience and faith. The word of the Lord declares: ***"Through Him we have received grace and apostleship for obedience to the faith among all nations for His name…" (Romans 13:5, NKJV).*** The Spirit of the Lord that lives in us moves us to obedience and faith in the word of the Lord, and teaches us to live with gratitude and favor in Christ Jesus. Strong March winds may blow and turn us in every direction, but I am determined we will not be moved from the love of Almighty God that is in Jesus Christ our Lord! Are you willing to fight the demonic winds of the enemy and experience great victory? The born-again child of God understands that in order to win you must fight! Allow each day to be a great day of victory as you fight against the enemy. Have confidence in the word that Almighty God speaks in your life. In doing so we will see and experience great promises from the Hand of our Lord Jesus Christ. I'm willing to see these promises, are you?

APRIL

Remembering God's Word Determines Your Spiritual Success

What You Plant in Faith Will Grow in Abundance (The Power of Communion)

> **"Most assuredly, I say to you, unless a grain of wheat falls into the ground and dies, it remains alone; but if it dies, it produces much grain." (John12:24, NKJV).**

In this New Testament scripture the Lord Jesus is referring to His death, burial, and resurrection. When He talks about the grain of wheat (corn in KJV) falling to the ground, dying and producing more wheat; He is referring to His crucifixion, death and resurrection that would occur to save all people from sins. Because of this one Man, Christ Jesus, many souls would believe, giving their life to the Lord, receiving the Holy Spirit, and cause more souls to believe and enter the kingdom of God. If you are so in love with this carnal life (the excitements of this world in which the devil places before you) you will lose your love for eternal life. The glamor of this world will overtake you and you will be drawn away from the eternal life promised by Almighty God. However, the person who hates his life in this world will keep his life for eternal life. Don't misunderstand me. I am not saying that a person should hate their lives that they should bring harm to themselves or despise their own flesh that they no longer want to exist on the earth. But when you are born-again by the water and spirit you understand the love of God dwelling in you. When you began to see the wickedness of this world, you will long for the kingdom of God. Remember what the Apostle Paul declared? ***"For I am hard-pressed between the two, having a desire to depart and be with Christ, which is far better. Nevertheless to remain in the flesh is more needful for you." (Philippians 1:23-24, NKJV).*** Paul understood that he had a great work ordained by Almighty God; and he could not go anywhere until the Lord God declared his time to be finished on earth. I believe we all wait with great expectation for that blessed day that we enter into the joy of the Lord at the coming of our Lord Jesus Christ! Our spiritual lives are being developed just as a flower bud is being developed in the soil below the ground. When the appropriate time arrives, the flower bud will spring up from the soil to a lovely flower filled with beautiful colors. Likewise as we mature in Christ Jesus others will admire the beauty of holiness that we possess through the Spirit of the Lord that is within us. It is a beautiful sight when the love of Almighty God shines through us and blesses someone's life. The light of God's countenance flows through us as we allow the Holy Spirit to work in us and through us, blessing the lives of others. We are the flowers that are sown in the earth and waiting to emerge from the ground. There is an expectance from us and others waiting to see the glorious beauty of these flowers. Have you ever considered the abundance of joy to see beautiful flowers coming up from the ground or these same cut flowers in a vase sitting in a living room? No matter where these flowers are, they will bring great joy to the sight and smell of many individuals.

I believe when Almighty God saves us, we are like the beautiful flowers that are in the ground or the flowers cut and displayed in a beautiful vase. Flowers are not grown in the ground to be left alone and never to admire its beauty. The glory of such flowers brings great joy to those who see and smell them. I believe we are like the flowers that the Lord has planted to grow up and bring great joy to others. The beauty of our lives is the love, joy, and peace that we bring to others. Think about this for a moment. When someone is sad or sick their loved ones will bring them flowers or fruit. Each flower or fruit is beautifully colored and has a unique wonderful smell that makes the recipient of these gifts very happy. The smell and the taste cannot be forgotten when the recipient receives these gifts and enjoy the sight and taste. Have you thought about allowing the spiritual buds of your life to be planted, grown, and distributed to others? There are so many people that are sadden by life conditions and waiting for someone to come with spiritual flowers to bring them great joy! Our world is void of such joy because the love of many has become cold. Even in the church the fruit of the spirit has dried up and become distasteful for many. Those of us with the Spirit of the Living God do not have to respond as the world that does not have the Spirit of the Living God. It does not matter how cold the world gets; we have the Spirit of Almighty God living in us. We do not have to respond, as the world does with a cold and unconcerned response to the spiritual need of others. When we see the needs of others the love of God in us motivates us to help others by attending to their needs. When others see the movement of God in us, they will honor the God in us and seek to do good even as we are doing the will of Almighty God.

As we walk with the Lord, we will experience the spiritual growth that the Lord desires. We become the spiritual gardens that grow up to a beautiful masterpiece that is well pleasing to our Lord Jesus Christ. We become like the flower buds planted in the fall and flower seeds planted in the spring to produce the beautiful flowers of spring and summer. I believe that our Lord Jesus Christ wants us to shine with all the glory that heaven has to offer, attracting every soul by the beauty of holiness within us.

Every flower is unique and beautiful in its own way. The Lord made us as each flower knowing that each of us is unique and beautiful in our own spiritual way. Our uniqueness will attract others that are attracted to the love, joy, peace and other fruit of the Spirit dwelling in us. The movement of the Spirit of Almighty God in us will allow us to bond with each other and help each other in the things of God.

We bond with Christ and one another in the sharing of communion. Each of us are taking part in one of the greatest rituals of the New Testament church. When we partake in communion we are acknowledging and showing the Lord Jesus' death until He comes back to earth to receive His church. There is a special connection between children of Almighty God that commune with others. The words declaring: ***"...Do This in Remembrance of Me," (1 Corinthians 11:24b, NKJV)***, is ascribed on the tables and vessels used in the communion service. Each time we partake of Holy Communion we remember the sacrifice that was made on our behalf to free us from the penalty of sin and grant us access into the kingdom of God. Communion is like watering and enriching the soil that holds the flowers we have planted. By God's grace we have been given the spiritual skills to cultivate God's garden and bring beautiful spiritual flowers and fruit into the lives of many. We learn naturally by repetitive action. Some type of repetition action fosters the greater percentage of what we learn. This is why every time we take communion there should be another step to our spiritual knowledge and success. When our spiritual success increases, we are able to deal with the adversity that will surely come into our lives. I think I've said it once before, a particular Christian faith got the communion part correct. Each time you enter the sanctuary communion is ready for you. Why are they doing this? They are obeying the scripture: ***"For as often as you eat this bread and drink this cup, you proclaim the Lord's death till He comes.*" *(1 Corinthians_11:26, NKJV).***

When we grow higher in the Lord, we will do better. I

believe in the written word that declares: ***"But grow in the grace and knowledge of our Lord and Savior Jesus Christ." (2 Peter 3:18a, NKJV).*** We grow when we see the favor of God on our lives. We will receive favor when we adhere to what the Lord has instructed us to do. Have we learned the things the Lord requires of us? Let's consider these things. Love Almighty God, love your neighbor, and stay away from sinful activities. When mercy impacts our lives, we grow to be beautiful and merciful towards others. When mercy, favor and knowledge fill up our lives we return this God given favor and show mercy towards others. When all these things are active in our lives my understanding of God's favor is activated in us and we move to a higher spiritual plain. Therefore, as we grow, we understand the death, burial, and resurrection of our Lord Jesus Christ to a greater degree. We become knowledgeable of the power that resides in Christ, and I am able to make more changes in my life and help others to make changes in theirs. But we cannot see what Almighty God is doing in us unless we take a good look at ourselves and a good look at the word of the Lord. We also must come to the conclusion that the Lord has put His Spirit in us to replace the ungodly nature we obtained from Adam. What's the ungodly nature? Adam's nature, and what do we replace it with? We replace the ungodly nature with the godly nature, the Holy Spirit and the word of the Lord. When I am aware of the glorious power that is dwelling in me, I am no longer afraid of the enemy. I realize I am equipped to fight and win! I understand that I am more than a conqueror. That means I win big! That means my success is great because when I speak the Name of Jesus, I am speaking power and I am speaking with authority! Please understand what the scripture declares: ***"Yet in all these things we are more than conquerors through Him who loved us." (Romans 8:37, NKJV).*** I am stuck on this scripture because it places me above the power of everything that wars against me. I am more than the things that come against me, I am more than just winning the battle, and I win big! We as children of God we win with great expectation and glory! We will win with great expectation and glory if we only believe and hold fast to the word of faith we have been given by the Lord.

Each time we take communion we are moving up the spiritual ladder of success. When we take communion, our spiritual nature should change to a greater height spiritually. I see things on a higher spiritual plain. My communication with Christ Jesus increases and my love for my neighbors and enemies increases to the point it blows my mind and the mind of others. It gives me great joy when the Lord God subdues my enemies and makes them overturn all the evil that they desire against me! Note what the scripture says: ***"For as often as you eat this bread and drink this cup, you proclaim the Lord's death till He comes." (1 Corinthian 11:26, NKJV).*** When we proclaim something we declare publicly, typically insistently, and proudly. When you began to proclaim something; you are reaching down deep within, and you are not ashamed to let the world know that I stand for this, and you cannot make me change my mind. Each time I take communion a change takes place. When I show the Lord's death, I am showing a sacrifice of great love. Each time I take and understand communion I am showing God's love and I am moving to a greater spiritual plain. I become more like Jesus and less like the old man. Each time I take communion there should be a spiritual change that takes place. My thoughts and actions towards the brother or sister I did not care for should be changing from dislike to a little fond of; from they are okay with me, to a sort of like them, to I love them even as God loves me. If you let God do it, your hate will change to love. And maybe by the time the Lord comes back, you will be ready to go back with Him. How well you remember will determine your success! How well will you remember what? The love, the sacrifice of Jesus' life, the power of His resurrection, and the <u>promise of His return</u>!

Let's consider a couple of important things pertaining to our salvation:

1. **The power of His resurrection** – no man since the fall of Adam had escaped the clutches of death. Only Enoch and Elijah were taken and did not see death. But Jesus did something that no other person could do. The Apostle Paul declared: ***"But God demonstrates His own love toward us, in that while we were still sinners, Christ died for us." (Romans 5:8, NKJV).*** When we could not get a prayer through, when we could not turn around and live a righteous life, Christ died but even more He was resurrected from the dead! Christ's resurrection slapped Satan in the face, put him in his place and read him the ultimate law from heaven. Consider what Jesus declared: ***"And Jesus came and spoke to them, saying, "All authority has been given to Me in heaven and on earth." (Mathew 28:18, NJKV).*** The enemy no longer owns God's people and he cannot do what he wills to them. We have Almighty God's given authority abiding in us through His Holy Spirit. We can speak and turn everything around that the enemy places before us. How did we get this authority? The infilling of the Holy Spirit! What did Jesus say? ***"But you shall receive power when the Holy Spirit has come upon you…" (Acts 1:8a, NKJV).*** The Holy Spirit comes to live in us and fight for us, and to ensure us the right to enter into the kingdom of God! We have a great promise from the Lord. I suggest we remember and use the promises of Almighty God to be a blessing to our lives and others. When we share these promises to others, and they receive them and share them with others we are doing a great work that pleases our Lord Jesus Christ.
2. **The promise of His return** – Jesus made a promise to us through the Apostle John: ***"And if I go and prepare a place for you, I will come again and receive you to Myself; that where I am, there you may be also. And where I go***

> ***you know, and the way you know." (John 14:3, NKJV).*** When I am aware of that special day of the coming of the Lord and I am reminded by the actions I take, I hold fast to what the Lord has said. When I make mistakes, I quickly make corrections and get back in fellowship with the Lord. Each day a greater awareness of the coming of the Lord is revealed. Consider the great love our Lord Jesus has for us. Would He make a promise to us and not keep it? I don't think so! What the Lord has declared in His word is surely coming to pass. I look forward to the movement of the Lord in the earth and spending eternity in the kingdom of heaven.

I am looking for that special day, the day that the Lord comes back to get His church! I'm not worried about what is left down here. I like the words to the song, *"When I see Jesus, amen!"* all of my troubles will be over, sickness, wars, and hatred will be over. I will be in a place where there will be no more death, pain, nor sorrow. Trouble will be no more, glory to Almighty God! Are you looking forward to that day? What a great day, a blessed day it will be indeed! Consider this old hymn: *Showers of Blessings:*

> *There shall be showers of blessings:*
> *This is the promise of love;*
> *There shall be seasons refreshing,*
> *Sent from the Savior above.*
>
> *Showers of blessing,*
> *Showers of blessing we need:*
> *Mercy-drops round us are falling,*
> *But for the showers we plead.*

Every born-again believer should hold fast to what the Lord has spoken to us concerning our lives. When Almighty God speaks to us, He is enriching our lives with His word that brings directions and blessings for our spiritual journey through life. I believe the Lord God is thrilled to overwhelm His children with good things that will encourage and support us on our journey through this life. I believe that most Christians have come to the conclusion that our natural lives can be difficult at times. But if we depend on the word of God, we will overcome the difficult times and enjoy the blissful times the Lord God has planned for us. There are some days that we become weary and long for Jesus' coming because of the evil conditions on the earth. As we approach the coming of the Lord, evil will become greater and greater. Nevertheless, it does not matter what the condition of the world is, we who are in Christ Jesus should remain faithful to loving the Lord and remain faithful to the word we have received from the Lord. Let's not forget the seed of righteousness that the Lord God has placed in us through His Holy Spirit. We are now able to accomplish the spiritual tasks that Almighty God desires that we should do to attract people into the kingdom of God. Our new birth and maturity in Christ Jesus give us a blessed place in the kingdom of God. We are empowered to tell others about the power of salvation through our Lord Jesus Christ and the wonder working power of the Holy Spirit working in us to spiritually inspire people to give their lives to Christ.

I believe it is time for all born-again believers to focus our minds on the coming of the Lord Jesus Christ and move away from the unlawful acts of sin. The word of God has declared that no one knows the day nor the hour when the Lord will return. It is imperative that we are ready when the Lord comes. Sin and unrighteousness have overtaken so many in this world that to acknowledge the Lord Jesus and the salvation at Calvary's cross is a foregone conclusion. Nevertheless, I cannot forget the sacrifice that was made at Calvary for the remission on my sins and the new birth process that gives me new life! I do not have a difficult time expressing to others the salvation that has come into my life. I cannot compare anything to the saving grace that the Lord our God has blessed me to receive. When I was first saved my pastor asked me how I was doing. I quickly expressed, *"All this and Heaven too!"* I was so happy that the Lord had saved me and had given me the greatest joy I had ever encountered. I was so amazed that God had changed and blessed my life that I continued to rejoice and be glad of all the things I had received from the Lord. I am sure most of you felt the same way when the Lord filled you with His Holy Spirit. Great love, joy, and peace has entered into your lives and nothing can be compared to it. The Spirit of the Lord that lives in me cannot be compared to anything on this earth. I am so happy, and I will rejoice even more when the Lord comes to receive His church. We are prepared for this day because of the great sacrifice that was made. Consider what the scripture declared: ***"...Without the shedding of blood there is be no remission." (Hebrews 9:22b, NKJV).*** Each time the remembrance of the crucifixion of our Lord Jesus comes there is a sadness in our hearts. Nevertheless when the remembrance of Resurrection Day comes shortly after there is exuberant joy because we now have hope to gain eternal life!

MAY

Phenomenal Growth - Unlimited Power In Christ!

"Consider the lilies, how they grow: they neither toil nor spin; and yet I say to you, even Solomon in all his glory was not arrayed like one of these. If then God so clothes the grass, which today is in the field and tomorrow is thrown into the oven, how much more will He clothe you, O you of little faith?" (Luke 12:27-28, NKJV).

The amazing power of Almighty God cannot be compared with anything on the face of this earth. In the previous scripture the Lord Jesus is referring to the amazing glory that is in the lilies of the field. Every flower that we witness is adored with great beauty that cannot be duplicated by the hand of man. The Lord God has arranged the beauty and glory of the flowers we see and smell. The Lord has allowed the wonderful smell to grace our lives and bring joy to our souls. It was the majesty of Almighty God that infused the wonderful sight and smell in the flowers that bring amazing peace to the person that enjoys the smell and sight that blesses their lives.

During the month of May every seed that has been sowed

and the plants that have been placed in the soil began to grow exponentially. The richness of the soil and the abundance of moisture from the April showers cause everything to grow beyond expectation. This phenomenal growth is caused by all these factors to bring about the fruit necessary for consumption. The gardener takes special care of these plants in order to reap the fruit that will be produced very shortly and the value it brings for sales and healthy consumption. It is amazing to watch the variety of fruit and vegetables grow so rapidly after being planted in the soil. Have you ever given thought as to the miraculous way the things that Almighty God has developed in the earth to grow and manifest through the soil? It is the Lord's doing and it is marvelous to watch the greatness of the Lord's work in the earth. These things that the Lord developed are satisfiable to our taste, and worth giving thanks, as we are partakers of the produce that gives strength to our natural bodies. We glorify the Lord for giving us the fruit of nature that we may eat and enjoy, but do we also partake of the fruit of the Spirit and enjoy for ourselves and with others? These things that the Lord spoke to us were spoken that the joy of the Lord may remain in us and that our joy may be full. This is life worth living and causes our lives to be filled with happiness! We ask this question because we are inundated with situations that allow us to come face to face with death, spiritual and natural confrontations. But I am convinced that the more we hear words of life the more we will speak life; and the more we speak life the more we will see the manifestation of life. When we see the great abundance of natural things growing and the beauty that it possesses, we rejoice and glorify our Creator for allowing the blessings of natural and spiritual substance to fill our lives. One of the most satisfying situations for a person or family is to be blessed with an abundance of things that satisfies the heart and soul. When there is an abundance of good things in our lives we rejoice and feel empowered to see even more of the manifestation of the blessings from Almighty God. We think about what got us into this position and we try to repeat the process for even more blessings. When blessings get even greater, we feel blessed and empowered to be a blessing to others. Our natural and spiritual blessings have similar meanings in our lives. In each case we rejoice and feel a sense of accomplishment. Let us consider the natural and spiritual accomplishments in our lives and give glory to our Lord God for the things He continues to do for us. When we consider all these wonderful natural and spiritual blessings, we will grow stronger in the Lord and receive blessings to distribute to others that they may see and give Almighty God the praise for the wonderful works that He does for His children.

Farmers of old, when they had a successful crop, they would repeat the process each year because of the blessing that was received. During my childhood I would watch my grandparents and parents take the seeds and plants and pray over them before placing them in the ground. My parents and grandparents would pay attention to the weather reports that the plants were not damage by the frost or animals that would cause harm. It seems that each year we had a successful year of production with our garden and fruit trees. Why were we successful with our gardens? We followed a book that was used to produce a successful garden, the *Farmer's Almanac.* Within this book there was the time to plant and the proper way to do specific agricultural tasks to ensure successful plant growth. When I consider the good natural things that were accomplished through the knowledge of wise men, how much more can we learn from the wisdom from the Lord our God? The Almighty God has the power to impart wisdom into the mind of man in order for him to be successful in all parts of life. If the Lord would do this for the natural man how much more would He do this for the man, He filled with His Spirit? Just as God gave the natural man the ability to create the *Almanac,* He has given the natural man the ability to become a spiritual man through the infilling of the Holy Spirit and the written word (The Bible). The Lord God has given us His word to lead and guide us into His great truth that will make us wise and spiritually powerful on earth and in the kingdom of God. The Bible serves as our spiritual *Almanac*, giving all of us the wisdom and knowledge to ensure the enrichment of our lives to be a blessing to Almighty God and to other people. The *Farmer's Almanac* serves as a source of information that helps individuals to grow and receive successful produce. Likewise, the Bible gives information to the nonbeliever and to the believer to increase in wisdom and strength and to accept the will of Almighty God that we might be strong in the Lord and in the power of His might. The wisdom of the Lord is great and powerful. The Lord God has placed so many things before us to learn what would make our life naturally and spiritually successful. Consider the book the Lord God has allowed us to receive, read, and learn that we might be spiritually successful in this life and in the life to come.

The Bible shines a great light in our hearts to recognize the things that are necessary to make us spiritually successful. The Bible is like the spiritual *Almanac* that gives us quality information for spiritual growth and success. When we consider the power of the written and spoken word of God, I am amazed and thankful that the Lord God chose us to be His children and be in the kingdom of God. Have you considered the spiritual wealth you have through salvation? Do not allow it to go to waste. Do you make the most of the spiritual wealth Almighty God had given us? The Lord has supplied so much for our spiritual enhancement. It is amazing what we can achieve if we abide in Christ Jesus. Consider the scripture: ***"As the Father loved Me, I also have loved you; abide in My love. If you keep My commandments, you will abide in My love, just as I have kept My Father's commandments and abide in His love." (John 15:9-10, NKJV).*** The key to our reward is abiding in Christ Jesus and adhering to every word that the Lord God has given us. Consider this, a seed cannot grow and produce fruit unless it abides in the ground. We cannot grow and obtain spiritual fruit unless we abide in Christ Jesus. Abiding in the Lord is the key to a successful spiritual life. I am determined to stay in Christ Jesus, not only will we have a blessed time on earth but think about the time we will have in Heaven!

Have you thought about having a wealth of spiritual power and authority; and yet being humble and filled with grace? We can do many things to accumulate wealth and power. Just less than a century ago some people gained wealth through agricultural means. People learned that wisdom and humility was a major factor in gaining and keeping wealth. Consider the word of the Lord: ***"The humble He guides in justice, And the humble He teaches His way." (Psalms 25:9, NJKV)*** and ***"Therefore humble yourselves under the mighty hand of God, that He may exalt you in due time, casting all your care upon Him, for He cares for you." (1 Peter 5:6-7, NKJV).*** Humility is one of the key factors in causing Almighty God to pour out His blessings, on His people. Again, consider the scripture: ***"But He gives more grace. Therefore, He says: "God resists the proud, But gives grace to the humble." (James 4:6, NKJV).*** Throughout the scriptures we are informed about the importance of humility in the life of a child of God. The Lord is welcomed to come into our lives and share the blessings that would make us spiritually and naturally wealthy. The Bible shares many examples of humility and spirituality leading to great blessing from Almighty God. Please consider what I am saying and witness what the Lord God will do for you.

Now let us consider our Phenomenal Growth and Unlimited Power from a spiritual perspective. Our humility means so much as we walk with Almighty God on the earth. We will see and experience things of great importance in our lives. The abundance of grace given to the humble believer makes a great impact in their lives and the lives of others. One of the things that stands out in the humble believer in Christ is the outpouring of Growth and Power In Christ that is seen by believers and unbelievers in the world. The humble believer receives favor, approval, acceptance, and goodwill from the hand of the Lord God and shares it with other people. When we experience such godly favor, our hearts are made glad and we reach out to others with the same measure of favor that has been given to us. When the growth and power of Almighty God abides in us, we cannot help but share this favor of Almighty God with others. When we see that our lives have been changed and the abundance of God's grace is being poured out on us, we are anxious to share this with others. It reminds me of the abundance of fruit and vegetables that would grow in our gardens. We had so much that we did not wait for someone to ask for something, we gathered the abundance of what we had and brought it to those who needed it or not. Just to see the look on their faces and the gratitude expressed made you want to do even more. Our spiritual lives should be similar. Almighty God has poured a measure of grace into our lives that we might be a blessing to others. Allow Christ to use you through the grace you have received. Many will understand the love of Almighty God and desire to receive the power of Christ in their lives.

Let's consider the power of Almighty God working in our lives. Every day that we are alive and well we enjoy the benefits of living, i.e. good food, romance, quality housing, and many other things that the majority of people consider good living. But when our good food spoils and causes food poisoning, romance turns into disagreement and fighting, and our neighborhoods turns from a utopia setting to a haven for cutthroats and thieves; our joy quickly turns into depression and life does not seem to be worth living anymore. The Lord said that these things would happen in our lives, therefore He made this declaration: ***"The thief does not come except to steal, and to kill, and to destroy. I am come that they might have life, and that they might have it more abundantly." (John 10:10, NKJV).*** When we really focus on this scripture and the promise of eternal life, we are not overwhelmed by all the negative things that will take place in our lives. It makes no difference how you look at it or how you try to figure it out; you will never be able to compare and declare natural life to be greater than spiritual life. Natural life has a determined end and spiritual life is a blissful time on earth and likewise for eternity in heaven! Spiritual life is filled with the joy that the Lord has promised. We must understand that whatever is the object of our focus and the desire of our dreams it will be the driving force to our destiny. If the object of our focus and the desire of our dreams is only natural or the greater percentage is natural, then the greater rewards of life is natural, and the spiritual part is minimal, and we are destined to fail. I believe that if we maximize our spiritual life the natural life will be beneficial, and we will enjoy our stay on earth until the Lord returns. Was this not the case with Israel? God informed Israel that if they put the Lord first, they would see the greatness of God in their natural lives. God spoke to the children of Israel through their leader Moses: ***"Now it shall come to pass, if you diligently obey the voice of the Lord your God, to observe carefully all His commandments which I command you today, that the Lord your God will set you high above all nations of the earth And all these blessings shall come upon you and overtake you, because you obey the voice of the Lord your God: "Blessed shall you be in the city, and blessed shall you be in the country. "Blessed shall be the fruit of your body, the produce of your ground and the increase of your herds, the increase of your cattle and the offspring of your flocks. "Blessed shall be your basket and your kneading bowl. "Blessed shall you be when you come in and blessed shall you be when you go out. "The Lord will cause your enemies who rise against you to be defeated before your face; they shall come out against you one way and flee before you seven ways." (Deuteronomy 28:1-7, NKJV).*** Wow, when we read this promise our hearts are overwhelmed and we are forever willing to receive the word from the Lord, follow His commandments and enjoy the riches of His grace!

The Old and New Testament scriptures give us the Unlimited Power In Christ! This unlimited power in Christ empowers every Christian to believe even greater the things the Lord has spoken. If Christ is speaking to you, you have power when you speak because Christ lives in you! We have the power to speak life wherever we are and to whomever we speak. What words are you speaking? If we speak words of life, we will see the manifestation of God's promises which will bring great joy in the lives of others and our life. Jesus spoke to His disciples declaring: ***"These things I have spoken to you, that My joy may remain in you, and that your joy may be full." (John15:11, NKJV).*** This is life worth living! We ask this question because we are inundated with situations that allow us to come face to face with death, spiritual and natural. But I am convinced that the more we hear words of life the more we will speak life. And the more we speak life the more we will see the manifestation of life. The Lord knows the condition of our hearts naturally, and the movement of the enemy to set us back spiritually. When we really focus on the scriptures and the promise of eternal life, we are not overwhelmed by all the negative things that will take place in our lives. It makes no difference how you look at it or how you try to figure it out; you will never be able to effectively compare natural life over spiritual life. Natural life has a determined end and spiritual life is forever! Remember, the object of our focus and the desire of our dreams, it will be the driving force to our destiny! What is your focus and what are your dreams?

Many children of God are failing because of a lack of understanding of the word of God. The sacrifice of our Lord Jesus Christ allowed us to be delivered from the penalty of sin. When we except Jesus death on the cross, and His resurrection from the dead, we place ourselves in a position to receive the Holy Spirit. When we receive the Holy Spirit and consecrate our lives to the Lord great changes take place in our lives. Consider what Paul said in the scriptures: ***"What shall we say then? Shall we continue in sin that grace may abound? Certainly not! How shall we who died to sin live any longer in it? Or do you not know that as many of us as were baptized into Christ Jesus were baptized into His death?***

Therefore, we were buried with Him through baptism into death, that just as Christ was raised from the dead by the glory of the Father, even so we also should walk in newness of life." (Roman 6:1-4, NKJV). Through the new life process we have been given the privilege to walk in Christ free of sin and prepare to enter the kingdom of God. While we are on this earth, we also have the privilege to receive natural blessings as we bear spiritual fruit that bring help to others. The Lord Jesus knew that it would be difficult to produce spiritual fruit if you did not understand how to produce natural fruit. Another reason Jesus said to His disciples the power of asking, seeking, and knocking was to enlighten them about the power of these attributes on earth and in the kingdom of God. When I walk in faith and I have confidence in Almighty God's word I do not have a problem asking. I feel like a son and not a servant. How does a son or daughter feel as opposed to a servant? I feel like looking because faith is ingrained in my spirit that I am going to find something and what I find is going to be worth something great! I am going to knock because faith tells me there's something great behind door number 1, 2, and 3! Behind every door is the blessings of our Lord Jesus Christ! He's just waiting to open the door as long as your entrance is led by faith! What is faith? Faith is a word from God that leads to a promise from God! Consider the scripture: ***"So then faith comes by hearing, and hearing by the word of God." (Romans 10:17, NKJV),*** and ***"Now faith is the substance of things hoped for, the evidence of things not seen." (Hebrews 11:1, NKJV).*** Faith comes as we hear what the Lord is speaking to us. It is important that every child of Almighty God know His voice and understands His word. Nevertheless, the written word of God (The Bible) and the voice of the Almighty is the ultimate contact we have with our Lord and Savior Jesus Christ. We learn the voice of the Almighty God as we walk with Him and learn the written word through the Bible. When we learn the written and the voice of the Almighty God, we will not be deceived by the voice of the enemy. Note the scripture: ***"My sheep hear My voice, and I know them, and they follow Me." (John 10:27, NKJV).*** It is imperative that every child of Almighty God learns the voice of our Savior. Our study and obedience to the word of God brings us into a new dimension that gives peace and tranquility in our spiritual lives; and allows us to obtain victory over the things of the enemy. Now let us consider one of the greater stages of our faith in Almighty God: ***"But without faith it is impossible to please Him, for he who comes to God must believe that He is, and that He is a rewarder of those who diligently seek Him." (Hebrews 11:6, NKJV).*** As a child of Almighty God, I do not dwell on the impossible or the negative. I may see what may be impossible for man but not impossible with Almighty God. And those things that are negative are removed from our lives by our faith and trust in the word of God's promise spoken to us.

As we grow up in grace and in the knowledge of our Savior Jesus Christ, we will see the greatness of our Lord perform marvelous things in our lives. Our spiritual lives will change for the best as we grow beyond the selfish and mundane things of this life. We will clearly see beyond the horizon of natural things and extend to the horizon of spiritual things that make our lives better and full of the grace that is extended to others that allow them to seek the presence of the Lord also. Each year I plant my natural garden during the early spring months. I expect a great harvest if I follow the prescribed book *(Almanac)*, that has for years contributed to great success. Thanks to Almighty God we have the prescribed book (The Bible) that for many years contributed to the spiritual success of many children of Almighty God. If you are not having the success you desire spiritually, look to Jesus, the Author and Finisher of our faith. We cannot obtain faith unless we hear the word of the Lord. Upon hearing the word of God faith is generated in our spirit. It takes faith to please God. Almighty God moves on our behalf when faith is alive in our spirit. It takes faith to move God! The spirit that the Lord Jesus has placed in the born-again believer desires communication with our Father. Upon new birth we realize that we have obtained spiritual life and membership in the kingdom of heaven. Consider the words Jesus spoke: ***"It is the Spirit who gives life; the flesh profits nothing. The words that I speak to you are spirit, and they are life. (John 6:63, NKJV).*** The words Jesus speaks are Spirit and they are Life! Just as following the *Almanac* will assure you phenomenal growth and greatness for your plants; our Lord Jesus Christ and the written Word will assure you Phenomenal Growth and Power in your spiritual life. When I read about the promises made by Almighty God and received by the children of God I am overwhelmed with joy! I believe that as a born-again believer I am in a position to receive such promises, if I obey God's word and stay in love with our blessed Lord Jesus Christ. Each of us that have received the Spirit of Almighty God are in a blessed position to ask what we will and receive from our Lord Jesus Christ.

I am convinced that there is nothing too hard for the Lord; and if we abide in Him and He abide in us we can ask what we desire, and He will give it to us. What a powerful promise from the Lord! I am holding on to the promises that the Lord God has made to me. I will not doubt or fear. I will be strong in faith and hold fast to the promise the Lord God made. As children of God let us be strong in faith and not wavering when things we have heard are promises from Almighty God. Remain patient and wait joyfully knowing that what the Lord has promised will come to pass. Many children of God are in the waiting stage and getting uncomfortable because of the long wait. However, I admonish you to hold on to the promise that the Lord God Almighty gave you. During my younger days as a Christian I would hear the older saints declare, "He may not come when you want Him but He's always right on time." This is a true statement and I will stand still and be patient until the Lord's promise is fulfilled.

JUNE

The Abundance of Growth

The tree grew and became strong; Its height reached to the heavens, And it could be seen to the ends of all the earth. Its leaves were lovely, Its fruit abundant, And in it was food for all. The beasts of the field found shade under it, The birds of the heavens dwelt in its branches, And all flesh was fed from it." (Daniel 4:11-12, NKJV).

During the month of June, the growing season abundantly brings forth much fruit. Each day when we inspect our garden there is new growth, fruit and vegetables ready to be harvested. During this time the gardener is overwhelmed and proud of the production of their garden. We take pride in what we have planted and the abundance of what has been produced. When we inspect our garden, we are so proud of the progress that we have made that we began to partake of the produce we have grown. Have you understood how proud the Lord God must be in the spiritual progress that we have made? We grew from a spiritual infant to the place where we are now. We were able to overcome many obstacles to obtain the spiritual growth that now resides in us. Remember the heavy rain, hail, and winds that cause us to think that our poor little seeds and plants would wash away? Since the maturing of our plants we are rejoicing even greater when we see the fruit of our labor. We have won several fights and we are willing to continue to fight the good fight of faith and win even more! Getting to the place where we are now has not been easy, but it has been worth the fight. Just like our spiritual fight, we have seen the abundance of spiritual growth that has taken place in us and we glorify the God of heaven for choosing us to be the ones that He uses to perfect His will in the earth. When there is an abundance of growth there is giving and sharing that makes the giver and receiver very happy. Consider when you have given someone something and how you and that person feel. There is a wonderful feeling within the giver and receiver. When there is an abundance of grace, and both parties share love within their hearts, we share with others this great feeling. It becomes obvious to us that love is poured out of our hearts and the giver and receiver is blessed by what is done.

When we are filled with the Spirit of the Lord, our God causes great changes to take place in our life if we allow it. When we are willing to continue allowing the Holy Spirit to move in us, we will witness phenomenal changes. The love of Almighty God becomes the greatest force in our spiritual and natural life. The movement of the Spirit of Almighty God in us allows great things to happen. Our maturity in Christ Jesus develops a great love in us for Almighty God, the people of God, and even the enemies that fight against us. Consider the scripture: ***"Love suffers long and is kind; love does not envy; love does not parade itself, is not puffed up; does not behave rudely, does not seek its own, is not provoked, thinks no evil; does not rejoice in iniquity, but rejoices in the truth; bears all things, believes all things, hopes all things, endures all things." (1 Corinthians 13:4-7, NKJV).*** How does it make you feel, or do you consider what the scripture says in ***1 Corinthians 13:4-7,*** impossible? I believe that the Spirit of Almighty God living in us, will give us the power to do what we should do in Christ Jesus. Many of the things that we (Christians) have the power to do comes from the Holy Spirit living within us. We have the power to do great things, but do we move into position to do them? There are many people that have the power to do great things but will not do them. Many Christians have the power of the Holy Spirit living in them but will not be moved to do the things that Almighty God is moving on their hearts to do. One of the greatest things that a child of Almighty God can do is to love and allow the love of the Highest to shine through them so other believers in the world can see, admire, and move to do such things also. Our abundance of love is shown through impossible natural and spiritual situations. Things that the natural person finds difficult or impossible to do will come easy for the child of Almighty God to do because of the Spirit of God dwelling in them. When the natural person considers ***1 Corinthians 13:4-7***, they may think that it is impossible to carry out this biblical task! Nevertheless, I have learned after many years that it is not difficult when we allow the Holy Spirit to work in us. I also know that obedience is the key factor in allowing the movement of Almighty God in the life of the believer. The natural gardener has learned that June is the time of the abundance of fruit and vegetables. It is also the time of the abundance of insects trying to attack and destroy our gardens. Since the attacks on our gardens are well known and documented, there are products natural and chemical that are well known to us to destroy the adversities against our gardens. A well-known statement often used is, "If you don't know ask somebody." Old and new farmers and gardeners from all over come to the hardware stores and read specific books on gardening searching for ideas to protect their crops. We buy all kinds of sprays and powders necessary to protect our precious plants that we have grown over a period of months, so one day these products will be sitting in our casserole dish, frying pan or at the state fair waiting to be eaten or judged. The success of our gardens is dependent upon our experience and or the knowledge of those in the gardening profession.

I believe similar knowledge applies to members of the household of faith. We do not know everything when we give our lives to Christ. Likewise, we do not know everything about spiritual walking and living for Christ when we get saved. Even after years of abiding in the faith there is still much to be learned for a successful walk in Christ. One of the key things we learn is how to fight spiritually and win against the enemy. Think about the scripture: ***"Be sober, be vigilant; because your adversary the devil walks about like a roaring lion, seeking whom he may devour. Resist him, steadfast in the faith, knowing that the same sufferings are experienced by your brotherhood in the world." (1 Peter 5:8-9, NKJV).*** Think about this scripture***, 1 Peter 5:8-9***, the words are quiet, calm and included to mean sober. Vigilant, means attentive and watchful. The words sober and vigilant are important in our walk with Christ because we cannot act any way or do whatever we desire to do. We are being watched especially by people who wish to disprove the power of Christian living and our belief in the Bible. Our sobriety and vigilance are a vital part of our Christian training and walk. When the devil seeks whom he can destroy he walks about as the natural lion seeking the weakest prey that he can attach and destroy. The roar of a natural lion strikes fear in the hearts of prey that are fearful of being destroyed. Therefore, the animals that are fearful will run with great anxiety trying to get away from the lion that is determined to take its life. Christians are informed in the scriptures: ***"Resist him, firm in your faith, knowing that the same kinds of suffering are being experienced by your brotherhood throughout the world"(1 Peter 5:9, ESV).*** Even though we may be under severe attack by the enemy, we stand with our confidence in Christ that we will win! The enemy will continue to come back, but I am confident we will win if we use the word of the Lord as our ultimate weapon. A great soldier or athlete has made up their mind to compete and win. They are determined that they will win and the enemy they are fighting will lose. Are you a great warrior willing to fight and win? Many warriors in Christ Jesus have made up their minds to fight and win the demonic battles that they are engaged. These battles are not easy but with complete confidence in Christ Jesus we will easily express, *"The battle is not ours but the Lord's."*

Let us also consider the scripture: ***"No one engaged in warfare entangles himself with the affairs of this life, that he may please him who enlisted him as a soldier. And also if anyone competes in athletics, he is not crowned unless he competes according to the rules." (2 Timothy 2:4-5, NKJV).*** The good soldier in Christ does not get involved in the things of this world. Such things take away the focus from spiritual things and the mission that has been ordained by the Lord. The enemy is cunning and very crafty getting the sons of God to focus on unrelated things while the important matters are neglected or hidden. Have you ever tried to repair something, and the attempt was unsuccessful because you had the wrong tool? Many times, in our attempts to overcome the attacks of the enemy, we are unsuccessful. Our lack of success is because we are fighting with our own words and not with the words of our Lord Jesus Christ. We are fighting spiritual battles designed to destroy the spirit that resides in humans. We cannot overcome these evil forces with natural weapons. We will never conqueror the enemy with our own natural ability. Only the word of God, prayer, fasting, believing, and faith are the powerful weapons that must be employed to win. If we are going to win, we must choose our weapons wisely and fight in the Spirit! I get great strength and power from Almighty God to defeat the enemy. The Spirit of the Lord that lives in us (the Holy Spirit), along with my brothers and sisters in Christ (the Holy Spirit in them), and the angelic forces that are dispatched to help in warfare is the forces that comes together to fight and win. Together we pull down strongholds, a place dominated by a particular group or marked by particular wicked characteristics. Consider the scripture: ***"For***

the weapons of our warfare are not carnal but mighty in God for pulling down strongholds, casting down arguments and every high thing that exalts itself against the knowledge of God, bringing every thought into captivity to the obedience of Christ, and being ready to punish all disobedience when your obedience is fulfilled. (2 Corinthians 10:4-6, NKJV). All godly forces come together to pull down and destroy the enemy! The enemy has demons to fight with him and for him, as well as humans that have rejected God and submitted to the will of the enemy. Nevertheless, the Lord has angels and humans that have submitted to His will and are willing to fight, knowing that the weapons we use are from Almighty God and nothing will overcome the power that is of the Lord our God! I want us to understand that we obtain great victories as a unit and not just as individuals. When we understand what we are fighting for and what we are fighting against as we will choose our God-given weapons and win. Note what the scriptures declares: ***"Therefore take up the whole armor of God, that you may be able to withstand in the evil day..." (Ephesians 6:13a, NKJV)***

Let's examine our spiritual warrior. God did not call us to salvation to use the old weapons that we utilized when we were in the world. The word tells us that our flesh is an enemy to God. We will never overcome demonic forces by our skillfully natural nature. We will never fight and defeat the enemy with the same tools that we once used in the world. Let me remind you that human hands do not make the weapons we use in spiritual warfare. The weapons we must use to overcome the forces of evil are mighty in God and are the only weapons that will pull down ungodly strongholds. Truth is a powerful spiritual weapon that defeats and destroys lies. The shield of faith is the only weapon that will deflect the ungodly darts that attempt to make us spiritually sick and bring us to destruction. The helmet of salvation is the only protection of warfare that will protect our minds and give us the right spiritual intellect to help us destroy the ungodly strategy used by the enemy. Our power in Christ is defined by what we know and how we use the power given to us by Almighty God. Let us be wise sons of God as we are approached by the enemy to destroy us. Christ living in us will destroy the works of the devil and continue to empower us to fight the forces of evil and win.

An athlete can know how to win a game, but it is their skills and actions that give them the victory. That's why the Apostle James declares: ***"Faith without works is dead!"*** In chapter one we discussed potential (stored) and kinetic (active) energy. If potential energy is never activated it has no purpose and it cannot be defined as useful. Kinetic energy (active) is defined as being active, having a purpose and will change whatever is around it because its force will generate change in whatever is in its path. I again ask you this question. Is your Holy Spirit power potential or kinetic? Is it just stored up and doing nothing or is it active and bringing about changes? Remember the scripture? "***For the weapons of our warfare are not carnal..." (2 Corinthians 10:4-6, NKJV).*** I am convinced that the Spirit of the Living God dwells in every believer as a kinetic spiritual force that we should use to destroy the works of the devil. Our weapons are mighty in God for reaping destruction on the devil's work against the people of God. I admonish every child of God to be confident in the word of the Lord, realizing you have power over the enemy as you fight the good fight of faith in Christ Jesus!

JULY

Unlimited Power In Christ! The Abundance of Growth in Mid-Summer

"The steps of a good man are ordered by the Lord, And He delights in his way. (Psalms 37:23, NKJV).

These things that the Lord spoke to us were spoken that the joy of the Lord may remain in us and that our joy may be full. This is life worth living and lives filled with happiness! We ask this question because we are inundated with situations that allow us to come face to face with death, and spiritual and natural confrontations. But I am convinced that the more we hear words of life the more we will speak life. And the more we speak life the more we will see the manifestation of life. I can declare this because Jesus said: ***"A good man out of the good treasure of his heart brings forth good; and an evil man out of the evil treasure of his heart brings forth evil. For out of the abundance of the heart his mouth speaks." (Luke 6:45, NKJV).*** It's easy to ask the question, "What's in your heart?" Sometimes we may not know what's in our hearts unless the Lord God reveals it to us. If we pay attention to what we say, and what we do we will understand the things that are in our hearts and make the necessary corrections to please the Lord and ourselves. I believe the believer in Christ has the pure heart that desires to live for God and walk in the beauty of holiness. It is the promises of Almighty God that we read and accept what will give us the unlimited power in Christ Jesus! Our spiritual growth and power come from the word of God. The word of God must be a part of our daily life. If we consider a great singer, musician, or athlete, we learn that the person becomes great because they give great time and practice to the talents that have been given to them. If Christ is speaking to you, you have power when you speak because Christ lives in you! I'm here to remind you as the Apostle Paul reminded the saints in Colossi: "...***Christ in you the hope of glory.***" **(Colossians 1:27b)**. We have the power to speak life wherever we are and to whomever we speak! What words are you speaking? The things we speak should be edifying not only to our brothers and sisters but also to all people. Our words in Christ have power to transform and empower lives. Have you spoken life to someone today? Have your words of life brought life and happiness to someone? When the words of Christ Jesus are spoken through us it will change the lives of people.

Let's consider the example of the abundance of good fruit and vegetables produced in the month of July. The harvest becomes plentiful and the quality of fruit and vegetables are at their peak. The produce is in such abundance that those who have large gardens and abundance of fruit trees began to can (preserve) the fruit and vegetables to be eaten and enjoyed months later when the gardens and trees no longer produce vegetables and fruit. I believe there are spiritual seasons in our lives that the Lord abundantly gives us words and actions that we can store up and released later. We use the words we have stored at the proper time to edify some and bring others into the kingdom of God. When we absorb the warmth and power of the Son of God great things will happen in our lives. We will be able to bless others as we have been blessed. The Lord can allow us to produce an abundance of good fruit that we may be able to share with other and have an overflow for ourselves. When we absorb the great power that is in Christ Jesus, we become more like Him! The grace of Almighty God grows in us and out of us into the hearts of others as we witness and share the love of God with others. What we see in others, grounded in Christ is the loving kindness and tender mercies that brings joy to those that are in our presence. Just as we see the natural fruit bless others and us, the spiritual fruit does the same. Notice what the scriptures have declared about the fruit of the spirit: ***"But the fruit of the Spirit is love, joy, peace, longsuffering, kindness, goodness, faithfulness, gentleness, self-control. Against such there is no law." (Galatians 5:22-23, NKJV).*** When you read ***Galatians 5:22-23;*** do you consider your spiritual worth in the kingdom of God? If God's Spirit is growing and working effectively in us, we as well as others will see the glory of Almighty God working in us and producing good spiritual fruit that benefits the kingdom of God. Let us take note of the first three fruit of the spirit, love, joy, and peace. The Lord placed these first three fruit in order of their notoriety, importance, and acceptance.

When love is present it draws attention and admiration. Even an infant child will understand the love that comes from the heart of a person. Love is the most unmistakable gift of the Spirit that refreshes the soul and gives great pleasure to those who give and receive it. We embrace love when it comes into our lives and we will do whatever we can do to hold on to it. We cherish love and express it that it may be expressed back to us. Love gives our hearts great pleasure and fills us with thanks and allows us to hold on to it as long as we can. I feel that there is no greater gift of the Spirit than love. Love attracts the broken hearted and heals those that cannot find healing from any other source. Love cannot be explained with the natural mind, but it is a healing source that is certainty welcomed. Love has everything to do with our salvation and the natural healing of our mind. Thanks to the Lord our God for giving us His Spirit that which includes the fruit of the spirit beginning with love. Love has everything to do with our salvation because it was love that allowed Christ to stay on the cross and shed His blood for the remission of our sins. If we want to understand real love, we must understand the great sacrifice that Christ made on the cross of Calvary. Christ shed His blood on Calvary and gave His life that even the worst sinner would have the right to acknowledge Jesus Christ our Lord and be saved.

The second fruit is joy. Joy as well as all the other fruit of the spirit is a very powerful attribute. When joy is present it changes our hearts from sadness and gloom to a state of happiness and contentment. Joy fills the heart with great pleasure that causes a person to smile on the inside and allow it to be reflected on the outside. Joy cannot be contained. It comes out no matter what conditions are around it. Joy is like the sunshine that burst through the clouds after a violent storm. Its brightness cannot be contained as every particle on the earth receives its light and warmth. When the joy of the Lord is present, we will feel the warmth of a smile and the feeling of great laughter. Joy comes to life when a baby or small child express smiles and laughter when something good happens to them. Even the person that does not know God seeks joy to be a part of their lives. Joy opens up new avenues to the soul, refreshes the spirit and causes our natural mind to be filled with laughter that satisfies the heart.

Last of the three-fruit mentioned is peace. Peace gives contentment and a satisfying calm to the heart of a person. It also moves on the heart bringing refreshment that gives a soothing rest to the soul. Peace is so refreshing that it causes the heart to relax and the soul to be at ease. If we were to explain all seven of the fruit of the spirit, we would understand the natural and spiritual benefits for our lives. When I consider what the Lord Jesus has given us through His Spirit my soul rejoices, and I am at ease because of what the Lord has allowed His people to receive.

Jesus wanted His fruit to live and remain in us when the Holy Spirit came upon us. These nine fruits would remain in us, and our lives would be satisfying to us and to those we meet. This is life worth living! We speak this because we are inundated with situations that allow us to come face to face with death, spiritual and natural. But I am convinced that the more we hear the words of abundant life the more we will speak, see, and live, the manifestation of a good life. As we said earlier, there are many things we enjoy in life that make our lives happy and joyful. Remember, we must understand that whatever is the object of our focus and the desire of our dreams it will be the driving force to our destiny! If the object of our focus and the desire of our dreams is only natural or the greater percentage is natural, then the greater rewards of life is natural, and the spiritual part is minimal. I believe that if we maximize our spiritual life the natural life will be better and worthwhile. This has been the case since man was created on the earth. God has informed His people that are abiding in Him that He would assure us the blessings of His covering and protection over our lives. Too many children of God are failing because of an obscured view of the word of Almighty God. Notice what the Apostle John said concerning the word of the Lord: ***"Abide in Me, and I in you. As the branch cannot bear fruit of itself, unless it abides in the vine, neither can you, unless you abide in Me." (John 15:4, NKJV).*** Many times after children of God have been born-again, we may forget that Father God has the ultimate authority in our lives. Yes, we can do many things independently, but as children of God we call for the help we need in Christ. Remember: ***I can do all things through Christ who strengthens me. (Philippians 4:13, NKJV).***

The Lord Jesus knew that it would be difficult to produce spiritual fruit if you did not abide in Him and trust the written and spoken word. Our faith becomes alive when we hear what Almighty God is saying. The word of the Lord teaches us to grow as the Lord speaks to us and as we read the written word of Almighty God. Similar to students in a classroom; when the subjects are being taught ears are wide open to receive knowledge. Wisdom becomes alive in our spirit and we continue to grow in grace and the knowledge of our Lord Jesus.

Jesus makes this declaration: ***"It is the Spirit who gives life; the flesh profits nothing. The words that I speak to you are spirit, and they are life." (John 6:64, NKJV).*** Do you want life? Many children of God are failing because the richness of the word of God may be absent from their lives. The word of God is manifest in our life as we embrace the word and have a love for Jesus Christ. Notice how love causes us to be alive and a well-being life towards others. When love is initiated towards others it grows beyond our expectations. When this happens a stronger bond of love is developed in our brothers and sisters, and in Jesus Christ our Lord. When this love is manifested in the body of Christ it gives evidence that new life is within us and we express the love of Almighty God. Our new life in Christ is evident by the activity of the fruit of the Spirit in our lives. New life abides in us through the infilling of the Holy Spirit. The Lord Jesus knew that it would be difficult to produce spiritual fruit in a natural environment. Therefore, He filled us with His Holy Spirit. The seed of spiritual life has been planted within us. As the seed sprouts it forms a plant that grows leaves, blossoms and eventually fruit. This is the natural concept of the bearing of fruit. However, if the plant is not cared for it will not bear much fruit or no fruit at all. The spiritual concept is similar to this. Almighty God fills those who request His Spirit to live in them. As we grow in grace and the knowledge of Christ, we speak to others about the saving grace of our Lord Jesus Christ. When many accept the word of the Lord and give their lives to Jesus, they will grow and produce fruit in abundance according to their faith and works in the Lord.

When we work spiritually with each other, we will see the manifestation of salvation enter into the hearts of many. It is analogous to the scripture that refers to one child of God planting, and another watering. Regardless, of who plants or waters, it is the Lord that gives the increase, or causes it to grow and bear an abundance of fruit. Now that I understand that it is the Lord all mighty that brings forth the fruit and seed within the fruit to bring more fruit, I rejoice before Almighty God for His great work in us and using every child of God to bring souls into the kingdom. Are you allowing Almighty God to work in you to bring souls into the kingdom of God? If you do, great things will be manifested in you.

AUGUST

When Things Remain Stagnant Stir It Up!

"Therefore I remind you to stir up the gift of God which is in you through the laying on of my hands. For God has not given us a spirit of fear, but of power and of love and of a sound mind. Therefore, do not be ashamed of the testimony of our Lord, nor of me His prisoner, but share with me in the sufferings for the gospel according to the power of God." (2 Timothy 1:6-8, NKJV).

You can add all the right ingredients for a cake but if you do not stir up the ingredients that are a part of the cake it will not be consistent nor rise to the level of perfection. The Apostle Paul as well as other writers of scripture tells us what we must do to be successful and what we must refrain from doing to ensure success. Some ingredients for success that we must include in our Christian walk are love, faith, and all the other fruit of the Spirit. We must also include determination and the ability to engage in spiritual warfare at any time. Fear must be left out of our spiritual walk if we are going to be spiritually successful. ***Hebrews 11*** gives us a thorough explanation of the examples of faith working in the believer. Each example in ***Hebrews 11*** starts out by saying, ***"By***

Faith," (in the ***NKJV***). Careful study of the scriptures indicates the Lord's spoken Word or His directions to those willing to receive and follow His word. The Lord through the Apostle Paul gave careful instructions to the believer to carry out to achieve spiritual success. When we believe and react to the word of Almighty God, faith is created and activated in us. The word that Almighty God placed in us must be activated and acted upon to satisfy the heart of our Lord. Notice the progression of faith in the hearts of the children of Almighty God. The Lord speaks, the person believes, receives the word the Lord spoke, and looks for what has been spoken to come to fruition. The person receiving the word from God makes a determination that what the Lord says will surely come to pass. Therefore, every child of the Lord that hears and believes the word of Almighty God will receive the specified promise. I believe that just believing is not enough. Notice the scripture: ***"You believe that there is one God. You do well. Even the demons believe—and tremble! But do you want to know, O foolish man, that faith without works is dead? Was not Abraham our father justified by works when he offered Isaac his son on the altar? Do you see that faith was working together with his works, and by works faith was made perfect?" (James 2:19-22, NKJV).***

Faith goes beyond just believing but believing and acting on what the Lord has spoken; believe what the Lord spoke, and act on what you heard. What if our father of faith, Abraham, had just acted on what he believed and left out the action that Almighty God was expecting to witness? Every child of our Lord Jesus Christ that is included in the heroes of faith, heard a word from God and acted on the word that they heard. This is why every child of the Lord must know the word, know when the Lord is speaking His word, and then act on the word to please our Heavenly Father. In the year nineteen ninety-seven the Lord spoke to me and told me to move from the Saint Louis area to the Maryland/Washington D.C. area and start a church. I knew it was the Lord speaking and my heart said yes, but I was unmoved until the Lord spoke again in nineteen ninety-eight. In nineteen ninety-nine I requested a transfer from the place where I worked in Saint Louis to a new job to the Maryland area. I found the house my wife and I desired, rented a large truck, packed and moved to the state of Maryland and began to work on my new job. After one year on my new job in Maryland I was blessed with a substantial raise. I was comfortable with every aspect of the move. However, the Lord spoke again saying, *"When are you going to do what I moved you here to do?"* I was troubled by the word the Lord spoke to me. Yet within three months I moved by faith and started the church with twelve people. The church grew as the Lord said. After fifteen years of successful ministry I turned the church over to my son, who is an ordained minister. The church is growing, and I am well pleased that I was obedient to the voice of the Lord. What if I had listened to the voices of many people telling me, I was making a great mistake by leaving Missouri? I would not be enjoying the blessings the Lord God has given to me during my twenty years in Maryland, and the contentment and peace that the Lord has given. The Lord removed the fear from my heart by overpowering it with faith!

Faith cannot work while fear is present. The scripture distinctly declares: ***"God has not given us a spirit of fear, but of power and of love and of a sound mind." (2 Timothy 1:7, NKJV).*** Since God did not give us the spirit of fear, why are we adding it to our spiritual walk? Almighty God assures us of three major attributes of His Spirit, power, love, and a sound mind! We, who understand how powerful we are in Christ, will also understand and show the faith that is in us through the Holy Spirit. When we allow faith to be embedded and work in us, we will witness the powerful acts of the Holy Spirit during great and wonderful things in our lives. When faith is active and fully functional your spiritual walk and mind is fully stable and anxious to do and see the wonderful works of God. We must remember, God did not give us the spirit of fear! There is a difference between the natural fear, which is a defense for the preservation of the body, and the spirit of fear, which is a device of the enemy used to destroy the spiritual energy that has been built up in the soul of man by the word of Almighty God. If spiritual fear resonates in your mind it will cloud any faith that was built up in your mind.

Fear creates a spiritual battle in our mind that fights against our faith. If the volume of fear significantly outweighs and overwhelm our faith, we will fail every time. Example: Joshua needed an extra shot of faith to take Moses place. Since Moses was dead, Joshua was chosen by the Lord God to lead the children of Israel through Jericho and fight and destroy those nations that they were instructed to do so. The Lord God appeared to Joshua as the Commander of the Lord's army. Some may wonder after all the instructions that Joshua had received why did the Commander of the Lord's army visit him. Note, Joshua was not given military instructions as in previous chapters. But Joshua was instructed by the Lord: ***"Then the Commander of the Lord's army said to Joshua, "Take your sandal off your foot, for the place where you stand is holy." (Joshua 5:15, NKJV).*** The command to Joshua was to remove his sandals and worship. Think about what was just done. After all the military instructions Joshua was commanded to worship. How often before a major decision, battle, natural or spiritual decision, we worship the Lord first and then we receive His instructions to advance forward? Our spiritual walk with Christ would be so much easier if we listen to the Lord's instructions and worshipped Him in spirit and in truth. Joshua's listening to Almighty God's instructions and his obedience in worship allowed him to be blessed in receiving the promises ordained by the word of God. Are you doing as instructed by Almighty God and worshiping and praising Him even before the battle is won? Sometimes we rely on our natural senses to obtain spiritual victories. I believe the Lord God is giving His children specific instructions to obtain the promises He has in store for us.

Joshua heard the word of the Lord and all the instructions that were given by the Lord. As the time came near to enter Jericho and the Lord instructed the fight, and he did exactly what he was instructed. We as children of our Lord Jesus Christ, are destined to receive the heavenly reward of our journey if we hear the word of the Lord and obey what we have heard, understand, and honor the Lord God with praise even before the fighting begins. Faith must overcome the fear that is trying to control us and keep us from receiving the promises that God has declared we should receive. Joshua was successful in his walk with Almighty God because he did not have the spirit of fear but move in the power of the Lord believing what the Lord had promised. Remember when the Apostle Paul made this declaration: ***"Therefore, my beloved brethren, be steadfast, immovable, always abounding in the work of the Lord, knowing that your labor is not in vain in the Lord." (1 Corinthians 15:58).*** Be steadfast, unmovable, and make great leaps and bounds in the work of the Lord when your faith is active, and fear is completely removed from your thoughts!

Saints and sinners will detect your work in Christ as you pour out the love of Almighty God to everybody. Also be at peace with everybody, joyful in any situation, happy with whatever situation God allows because the word of the Lord assures you that Almighty God will see you through. So, I say to this body of believers, let Almighty God be seen and be active in your upcoming future. The fruit of the spirit that lives in you let it grow and manifest! Do not allow your fruit to become dormant or spoiled. Stir it up and enjoy for others and yourself! Let this be one of the best spiritual years of your life. Let this year be the year that you are healed, delivered, set free, and bountifully blessed! If you cast out the fear and allow the fruit and gifts of the Spirit to flourish in your life, you will see great things that you will remember the rest of your lives! There are acts of faith that have happen to me all during my saved life. I cannot forget all these wonderful things that the Lord has done. When I remember these things, I am encourage moving as the Lord God instructs and witness great things happen in my life.

Are you willing to see great things ordered by the Lord God in your life? If so, stir up the gifts that Almighty God has placed in you. I believe that whatever spiritual work the Lord has ordained for us to do we will receive a reward for the work we have done. We were not saved just to sit around, occasionally go to church and never actively do the work that God is calling us to do. I have found that the work the Lord has committed for me to do is the most rewarding things in my life. I find that when I actively engage in the work that I have been instructed by the Lord I am excited and joyful to be call by Almighty God to work in His vineyard. When I see the increase of souls being saved and edified by the teaching of the word of the Lord my soul rejoices and I am willing to do more to help enhanced the kingdom of God. I will say as the Apostle Paul declares, again: ***"I planted, Apollos watered, but God gave the increase."*** ***(1 Corinthians 3:6-7, NKJV).*** So then neither he who plants is anything, nor he who waters, but God who gives the increase." My heart rejoices because Almighty God allows us to do something in His kingdom. I pray that every child of God will become active in the work that the Lord is calling you to do. Move by the active faith that the Lord has placed in your heart and witness the great blessing that will come into your life!

SEPTEMBER

A New Season – Special Session

Anticipating The Coming of the Lord

"But I do not want you to be ignorant, brethren, concerning those who have fallen asleep, lest you sorrow as others who have no hope. For if we believe that Jesus died and rose again, even so God will bring with Him those who sleep in Jesus. For this we say to you by the word of the Lord, that we who are alive and remain until the coming of the Lord will by no means precede those who are asleep. For the Lord Himself will descend from heaven with a shout, with the voice of an archangel, and with the trumpet of God. And the dead in Christ will rise first. Then we who are alive and remain shall be caught up together with them in the clouds to meet the Lord in the air. And thus, we shall always be with the Lord. Therefore comfort one another with these words." (1 Thessalonians 4:13-18, NKJV).

Since the ascension of our Lord Jesus Christ the church has been talking about the coming of the Lord to take His people to glory. In this twenty-first century when we are informed about the coming of the Lord Jesus, we gladly anticipate the Lords' coming. However, as time lingers on there seems to be less talk and excitement about the Lord Jesus' return to take His people to glory. If we take a close look at the way our world is changing, we should have a greater interest in the what the Lord has said about His return. Have you notice the change lately? Let's consider a scripture: ***"But know this, that in the last days perilous times will come: For men will be lovers of themselves, lovers of money, boasters, proud, blasphemers, disobedient to parents, unthankful, unholy, unloving, unforgiving, slanderers, without self-control, brutal, despisers of good, traitors, headstrong, haughty, lovers of pleasure rather than lovers of God, having a form of godliness but denying its power. And from such people turn away." (2 Timothy 3:1-5, NKJV).*** It's very interesting that this epistle and some of the others were by the Apostle Paul between 90 and 140 A.D. This information informs us about the future when the Lord would return and take His church out of the earth. If we pay attention to what is being said in ***(2 Timothy 3:1-5, NKJV),*** we will witness the wicked activities taking place all around us. Such wickedness occurs in our homes, schools, and on our jobs. Murders are increasing as people are fighting against each other. Information is increasing as new drugs are being developed to alter the minds of individuals. Families are fighting and killing each other as mind altering drugs are prevalent in the lives of our families. When someone tries to do good, they are met with resistance by others to do evil and even go as far as harming others. It is obvious that many people are out of control and care less how they treat others. Many people have turned away from God to do whatever they desire to please themselves regardless of their spiritual downfall. The scriptures declare that the love of many has grown cold. People are not respectful of one another and selfishness has grown to an all-time high. Have you seen some of these things occurring in the world? I'm sure you have, and things seem to be getting worst. One of the greatest driving forces behind this movement of evil is the love of money and the things it can do to enhance our lives, good or evil. The Bible declares: ***"For the love of money is a root of all kinds of evil, for which some have strayed from the faith in their greediness and pierced themselves through with many sorrows." (1 Timothy 6:10, NKJV).*** People are doing mental and bodily harm to close relatives and friends to obtain money and drugs to satisfy their addictions and desires to be rich or intoxicated or both.

All these things are driving us further from our love for Almighty God. But what about those who are not addicted to drugs and alcohol? People are working long hours to gain large sums of money to increase wealth and have material things. This has cause many to walk away from Almighty God for the material things in life. The material things in life have become much more important than the spiritual things that are being offered to secure our place in the kingdom of heaven. Have we considered that these material things are only temporary? We spend large sums of money for a car that can easily get in a serious accident and be destroyed. Or what about the fancy clothes we purchase and suddenly they are eaten by moths. When we consider these things, we come to the conclusion that everything is temporary, even the life we live. Don't misunderstand me, I believe Almighty God has placed these things on earth to bless His children with pleasure and enjoyment. But these material things will never replace the salvation Almighty God has given to us. Let us consider the words of our Lord Jesus Christ: ***"I know your works, that you are neither cold nor hot. I could wish you were cold or hot. So then, because you are lukewarm, and neither cold nor hot, I will vomit you out of My mouth. Because you say, I am rich, have become wealthy, and have need of nothing'—and do not know that you are wretched, miserable, poor, blind, and naked—"***

(Revelation 3:15-17, NKJV). Our Lord Jesus was speaking to the angel (pastor) of the Laodiceans church. The Lord witnessed their love for money and their increased riches that led them to stray away from salvation that was given to them. If we consider what had happen to the Laodicean church, we can easily see that this same spiritual degradation is happening today. Some biblical scholars have determined that the Laodicean church is the church on the earth just before the coming of our Lord Jesus Christ. When we witness what is happening to the church, the desire for money and the love for our brothers and sisters has decreased. We are almost certain that we are in the Laodicean church age. If this is true should we not adhere to the scripture that declares: ***"Therefore, brethren, be even more diligent to make your call and election sure, for if you do these things you will never stumble; for so an entrance will be supplied to you abundantly into the everlasting kingdom of our Lord and Savior Jesus Christ." (2 Peter 1:10-11, NKJV).***

When we hear about the coming of the Lord, we may become excited for a moment, but we soon shift back to our day to day activities and forget that the Lord has informed us through His word ***(I Thessalonians 4:8-11, NKJV)*** that He would return and take His people out of the earth. We are instructed in ***(Revelation 3:14-22, NKJV)*** that we live in the last stages of the church. The Bible has informed us that the church would be neither cold nor hot but lukewarm. We are experiencing this as we see the body of Christ decrease in its excitement for the things of Almighty God. The church should be preparing for the coming of the Lord with great joy and excitement. When we witness Bible prophecy being fulfilled it is a reminder for us to get ready and stay ready to witness the coming of the Lord. Have you witnessed the turmoil and corruptions in our government, churches, and other important public organizations? Open your eyes to the evil things that are taking place in our world. These major organizations should be examples of dignity and truth but have drifted away from their righteous calling to organizations of selfishness and corruption. When I witness these things, I am spiritually motivated to get ready and prepare for the coming of our Lord Jesus Christ. We cannot overlook all these unrighteous things that are going on and the affects they are having on human nature and our world. The Lord has called us to salvation, let us obey His Word and allow the Holy Spirit to work in us the righteousness that the Lord desires so we may be pleasing to the Lord. I am determined to witness the return of our Lord Jesus Christ and go with Him to glory. It is important for the children to stay well established in Christ and never look back into the world that the Lord brought us out of. The return of the Lord Jesus will be one of the most important events for the child of Almighty God.

We are blessed with some of the best living conditions ever. Great modes of transportation, good jobs, and the best and abundance of foods are common things in most of our lives! Please do not misunderstand me. God is allowing us to be blessed with all these things. However, as we enjoy all these blessings please do not forget our Lord Jesus Christ who came to earth, and willingly gave His life that we may have eternal life! Now is the time for the children of our Lord God to expect and prepare for the Lord's return. I know I am repeating the coming of the Lord often in this book. However, I want each reader to get the message of the Lord's return and make preparation. When Jesus ascended into the heavens His disciples were looking up into the heavens, and two men spoke to them and reminded them that as they have seen Jesus leave, He is coming back in the same manner. The Apostle Paul reminds us that the Lord is coming back for His Church, the Body of Christ. Do not forget that we are the church. We are His Body and at the coming of the Lord we will soon become His Bride! Since we are in this church age and it is clear that the church has become lukewarm. Remember to remove yourselves from being lukewarm and switch to the hot mode! In doing so you will see the glory of Almighty God and be ready for the coming of the Lord! Jesus declared: ***"Behold, I stand at the door and knock. If anyone hears My voice and opens the door, I will come into him and dine with him, and he with Me. (Revelation 3:20, NKJV).*** Jesus is knocking on the doors of each of our hearts. He wants each of us to come back to our designated place in the Body of Christ and enjoy the sweet communion that we once shared with Him! There are so many things in this life that have distracted us from expecting the return of the Lord. The variety of worldly activities has pulled many away from our love and commitment to Christ and allowed our minds to drift away from salvation and the love we once had for the Lord Jesus. Nevertheless, Jesus has given us the power to overcome whatever has pulled us away from Him. He continues to call us by name urging us to come back to Him and experience the glory that we once shared with Him and the other members of the church. Note Jesus' declaration in the scriptures; ***"To him who overcomes I will grant to sit with Me on My throne, as I also overcame and sat down with My Father on His throne. (Revelation 3:21, NKJV).*** The Lord has given us that overcoming power through the Holy Spirit. The Holy Spirit that is dwelling in us will give us the power to overcome every evil force that has moved us to that lukewarm state. Are you ready to overcome the lukewarm state and become hot again for the things of God? There is an old song that remains in my heart since I gave my life to the Lord…

Oh, I Want To See Him

Oh, I want to see Him, to look upon His face,
there to sing forever of His saving grace.
On the streets of glory let me lift my voice
Cares all pass home at last ever to rejoice.

Throughout this book we talk about how we should live during the seasons of the year. I felt led of the Holy Spirit to commit this month to be aware of the coming of the Lord. We get involved in so many things that we may forget that the Lord Jesus Christ will soon return to take His church out of the earth. Just like we prepared ourselves to plant and develop a great garden, likewise it is very important that we do likewise spiritually to be ready to meet the Lord Jesus in the air. I feel that the coming of the Lord is the apex of the salvation we have embraced on the earth until the glorious time we will experience in heaven. Just as the planting of our gardens that we treated so well to see the glorious fruit and vegetables; we should likewise treat our Lord Jesus Christ with love and respect for the great salvation we have received and our entrance into the kingdom of heaven. There is no greater love than the love the Lord has for us than to give His life as a sacrifice for our sins. Jesus also rose from the dead and gave us the Holy Spirit ensuring us the power to live free from sin. Each day we live we are empowered by the Spirit of the Living God to live in holiness with our Lord Jesus Christ. Although many things cross our path to discourage us and cause us to think negatively about the promises that the Lord God has given us. Many things will cross our paths to discourage us causing us to be downhearted. Nevertheless, if we remind ourselves of the future promise for all saints of the Highest, we will not allow the negative things of this world to get us down. When I think about the streets of gold, the walls of jasper, and the gates of pearl and the many other glorious things that our Lord Jesus has prepared for His Bride, I rejoice with joy unspeakable and full of glory! We will not see or experience the evil that will be encountered on the earth. Our joy will be complete, and we will live for eternity with our Lord Jesus Christ! When I think about the coming of the Lord, leaving this evil earth and living in the blissful conditions described in the Bible, I rejoice with great expectation to see that day coming.

One of the old songs during my youth expresses the thoughts of my heart even unto this day.

Joy Unspeakable and Full of Glory

I have found His grace is all complete,
He supplieth every need;
While I sit and learn at Jesus' feet,
I am free, yes, free indeed.

Refrain:
It is joy unspeakable and full of glory,
Full of glory, full of glory;
It is joy unspeakable and full of glory,
Oh, the half has never yet been told.

It's been almost fifty years since the Lord filled me with His Holy Spirit. Yet I have not grown tired of waiting for the Lord's return and to receive His children to glory. Others as well as I continue to express thanks for the salvation that has entered into our lives. We also wait with great anticipation of the Lord's return with all the glory and honor that will be upon our lives! I suggest that none of us grow tired of waiting for our Lord's return. What a great day that will be! All the things that troubled our soul will be over and we will enjoy the joy of the Lord forever.

My thoughts about the vegetables and fruit are similar to the coming of the Lord. In our vegetable gardens a seed is planted, and the seed grows until it is ready to produce fruit. When the fruit is ready the farmer picks the fruit and rejoices for the quality increase he receives. Consider the word of the Lord I have previously quoted of the Apostle John: ***"Most assuredly, I say to you, unless a grain of wheat falls into the ground and dies, it remains alone; but if it dies, it produces much grain." (John 12:24, NKJV).*** The words of ***John 12:24*** speaks directly to the spiritual death of our Lord Jesus Christ and His resurrection from the dead to bring life to so many more. Our Lord Jesus Christ gives this great example that also applies to us who are created in

His image and willing to pass from death to life by being filled with His glorious Spirit. Nevertheless, it is imperative that we die naturally and be born again to carry out the labor that our Lord Jesus has determined for our lives. It is imperative that as we grow in Christ that we gladly produce much fruit in the name of our Lord Jesus that we bring great joy and victory to our brothers and sisters. Also consider the words of the Apostle Paul: ***"Therefore we were buried with Him through baptism into death, that just as Christ was raised from the dead by the glory of the Father, even so we also should walk in newness of life." (Romans 6:4, NKJV).*** Our resurrection in Christ gives us great power and glory to do wonderful spiritual things in the earth. Many will see our wonderful works in Christ and glorify Almighty God in heaven. We must never forget our identification in Christ. We have been filled with the Holy Spirit of promise that assures us the right to the tree of life.

Let us consider all the promises that Almighty God has given us and offer the praise of thanksgiving for the abundance of blessings we have received. When we see all the things the Lord has given and our gift of eternal life our hearts should be filled with joy unspeakable and full of glory! Have you seriously considered the return of the Lord and going back with Him when He comes? I am holding on to my faith and expecting a great time with my spiritual brothers and sisters in the kingdom of heaven. I believe the Lord has so much more for us to accomplish naturally on earth and spiritually in the heavens. Let's leave our cares of the flesh behind and seek after those things of the Spirit. The Lord God has so much more in store for His children. Let's come together in unity and express the love of God in our hearts. I believe we will experience so much more, we will be edified, and the Lord will be glorified!

❖ ❖ ❖

OCTOBER

The Harvest Continues

Praising God For The Abundant Harvest

(Psalms 107:33-37, NKJV)

There He makes the hungry dwell,
That they may establish a city for a dwelling place,
And sow fields and plant vineyards,
That they may yield a fruitful harvest."

During our season of plenty we give Almighty God the praise for allowing so many wonderful things to grow and be a blessing to our families. We are overjoyed by the abundance of produce that has blessed our tables and the things that have filled our storage for the future. There is nothing better than to see the blessed results of your labor that will serve as a great blessing for the present and the future. Whenever an abundance is achieved, we will acknowledge the blessing and glorify Almighty God for allowing great things to be in our lives. One of the things that we immediately understand that if it had not been for the blessings of the Lord, we would not have achieved the abundance that we have. Many farmers throughout the United States celebrate a special time in the autumn called Harvest Home Coming. This is a time of celebrating the abundance of produce achieved by farming. Great celebrations take place remembering the great success that was achieved during the gardening season. Each year celebrations are performed to remember the successful harvest that took place that year. It does not matter if one year has greater success or another, a celebration takes place to remember the success of that year and for the year that follows.

Celebrations like Harvest Home Coming and others give the farmers and gardeners a measure of hope for the next year. The belief in the special guide to farming, The *Almanac*, and trust in the power of the Almighty, gives the farmer and gardener hope that the success of the garden would be in the Hands of the Lord our God. If the farmer didn't have faith in God, he or she would worry and be concerned about planting a garden each year. They would also not have faith in the *Almanac*, that in many cases rely on weather conditions and scientific data to forecast specific conclusions. Our walk in Christ could have similar meanings to that of the farmer and the *Almanac*. When God saves us, it is not just for us to enjoy and embellish for ourselves. Almighty God saves us to be a witness to others and that those we have witness to will eventually give their life to Christ and do great things in the kingdom of God. The Lord God saved us that we might speak life to others that they might embrace salvation and keep passing it on to others to receive and enjoy. When a farmer or local gardener takes their prize produce to market or for competition to be judged they are extremely proud hoping they will receive a prize or special commendation for the hard work they have done to grow the fruit they are presenting. Our life in Christ should be somewhat the same way. The Lord Jesus works diligently with His children to ensure that we grow in grace and in the knowledge that He is giving to us. I believe the Lord God is so very pleased when He see us grow spiritually. Also the Lord is pleased when we overcome the things that are used to negatively impact our lives are no longer affecting us. Our spiritual lives have a great impact on others as they give their lives to Jesus and obtain the wonderful salvation! Most people don't know what they are missing until they embrace the Lord's love for their lives. There is so much joy that is missing if we refuse God's love that He willing offers.

Most people don't realize the joy that they have received until they give their life to Christ and receive the abundance of joy that is in Holy Spirit that is living in them. The Lord changes our lives through the new birth process. Our whole life changes and new spiritual things come to us making our life worth living. The Lord God gives us so much that sometimes we feel overwhelmed by the blessings we receive. Nevertheless, just as the blessings we receive the praise should flow from our lips. We honor the Lord for our salvation and for the many things that expresses the tone of the upright before the Lord. Consider this scripture: ***"Rejoice in the Lord, O you righteous! For praise from the upright is beautiful." (Psalms 33:1, NKJV).*** Just think how the Lord feels when praise flows from our hearts and our lips. We honor the Lord God with praise for the wonderful things the Lord has done for us. The Lord God considers our praise to Him most beautiful, wonderful, and pleasant to His ears. Have you ever thought why David was considered a man after God's own heart? Consider the scripture: ***"And afterward they asked for a king; so, God gave them Saul the son of Kish, a man of the tribe of Benjamin, for forty years. And when He had removed him, He raised up for them David as king, to whom also He gave testimony and said, I have found David the son of Jesse, a man after My own heart, who will do all My will." (Acts 13:21-22, NKJV).*** Wow, what a wonderful statement from the Lord! Almighty God had found a person, after His own heart that would do all His will! Just think, the Lord was well pleased with choosing David because David sought the heart of God desiring to please the Lord. Even when David committed adultery with Bathsheba and once she was pregnant, David had her husband Uriah killed, David repented of the wrong he had done and accepted the penalty the Lord imposed on him for his sin. There may be things in our lives that we have done to dishonor the Lord our God. I have learned through the actions of David, king of Israel, honor the Lord with all your heart and if you sin, repent and allow the Lord to cleanse your life and commit to living a life free of sin.

The members of the body of Christ must be an example of the righteousness of the Lord God by obedience and acting on the scriptures that we find in the word of God. We must first be honest with the Lord, ourselves, and others if we are to speak and act honestly with the world about the salvation of our Lord Jesus Christ. People are watching us when we declare we are the righteous seed of God Almighty. The ability to turn others from sin to righteousness is dependent on the love we show to each other and to Almighty God. As a body of believers, we are also witnessing and providing the world with an example of Christianity, that gives hope and joy for the salvation available through Jesus Christ. Remember, we are a body of believers that are unified by our gifts and talents that bring glory to the Lord our God. One of the major reasons that Almighty God brought us together is to share the works He has given us to the glory of the kingdom of God. Our spiritual design is to work together, fight together, and see God's glory together! I see our victory as we work together in the kingdom of God bring down the kingdom of darkness and not bring down each other. We may be yet individuals, but we are united together with each other and with Almighty God. We have become an unstoppable force in the earth as long as we maintain our unity. We will become a highly blessed and favored people as long as we are unified in the Spirit! The enemy would love to stop us by keeping us from uniting with each other and doing things together that enhances the kingdom of God. As long as we are united together in Christ, we will always be victorious! Therefore, I want you to understand that when you come together to celebrate the death of Christ, which gave each of you your spiritual life, leave the schism out of the house, leave the separation and segregation out of the house of God and our individual houses. If you want to see a greater manifestation of Almighty God's blessing, treat your brothers and sisters the same no matter what their social/economic status! Together we can stand against the separation and schisms to form a powerful unity that will evoke positive change and generate the real love of Christ! Real love will allow you to be kind to everyone, giving when there is a need, and picking up those that may have fallen down! But we must remember the real love that brought us into salvation! Jesus Christ died on Calvary's cross to save us and give us the power to come together and enjoy the blessings of salvation. Solomon wrote: ***Though one may be overpowered by another, two can withstand him. And a threefold cord is not quickly broken." (Ecclesiastes 4:12, NKJV).*** Throughout the scriptures we are often reminded about the power of unity. When we are in unity there are great things we can accomplish. Just think, if we can do this in the natural think of even greater things in the spiritual. The Lord has given us the power through His Holy Spirit to give us the strength to overcome all obstacles and obtain victory in the Name of our Lord Jesus Christ. Have you considered the power that is in each of us as born-again believers? It is amazing and we have not come close to using the Holy Spirit potential that dwells in each of us. I believe we have not come close to using the spiritual power that resides in us. When we work together in spiritual unity, we can experience even greater spiritual power. I believe the Lord has so much more for us to accomplish spiritually and naturally when we work together and become a three-fold cord as mention in ***Ecclesiastes 4:12***. Let us leave the cares of the flesh behind and seek after those things of the Spirit. The Lord God has so much more in store for His children. Let's come together in unity and express the love of God in our hearts. I believe we will experience so much more, and the Lord will be glorified!

The last several months we have discussed the growing season for plants and vegetables. As we enter the autumn season there are a few plants that will continue to grow through the autumn and winter season. During the month of October some of the fruit and nut trees produce the wonderful produce that enrich our lives. It seems as though the Lord God gives us an abundance of things throughout the year to satisfy our taste and nutrition. Even after the abundance of fruit and vegetables have gone away, we still have plenty of other things to be a blessing to our taste and health. The Lord knows just what to do to satisfy the heart and taste of mankind. The Lord God never leaves us without the necessary things to be a blessing to His children. Just as the garden and fruit trees that gives us great foods throughout the year, we are blessed with great spiritual things throughout our time on earth to give us the spiritual blessings to get us to the next level. Just as the growth of our natural gardens are important to us, so is our spiritual growth. There are spiritual times and seasons in our lives that are very important to our spiritual growth. There are times when we collect an abundance of things to be used later in the season or even years later. The Lord God will give us words of wisdom that are to be used many days later to bless the lives of others and ourselves. It is important that we consider this concept. Every spiritual word may not be for us but for someone that is in need of spiritual or natural comfort to get them through the next day or month. Remember, we are the body of Christ, working together to produce great spiritual things that will edify our brothers and sisters. Consider the word of the Lord: ***"For as we have many members in one body, but all the members do not have the same function, so we, being many, are one body in Christ, and individually members of one another." (Romans 12:4-5, NKJV).*** The Lord God made each of us different with a variety of gifts and talents that will be a blessing to each other and the kingdom of God. We are one body with many members, helping one another to accomplish the spiritual task that the Lord God has designed for each of us.

Remember, there are spiritual acts as well as times and seasons that occur in each of our lives. Take advantage of everything that God allows in your life. The Lord has a purpose for every situation that occurs. I am often reminded of this scripture; ***"And we know that all things work together for good to those who love God, to those who are the called according to His purpose." (Romans 8:28, NKJV).*** I believe the Lord has a good purpose for everything that occurs in our lives. Such things will cause us to grow and produce good spiritual fruit. Allow the Lord to work these things and your life and we will be bountifully blessed, enjoying the fruit of your spiritual and natural labor, and the Lord God will be glorified, and we will be satisfied.

NOVEMBER

Celebrating The Day of Thanksgiving

One of the most festive times of the year is Thanksgiving! People get together to see friends and relatives they have not seen for many months and even years. The story is often told about the people who came to the United States from other countries that shared a meal with the people who lived here already. The two or more classes of people decided to come together and share a meal with each other striving to put away their differences and have a moment of peace as they gathered with each other. Many centuries later this same concept still exist. Thanksgiving seems to be the time that many just want to get home and enjoy the warmth of kinship and bonding with friends and family. Even during this time, love between family members has rekindled into lasting relationships, bring families closer and working together to form a united bond for greater things. Many families around the world have discovered that the bond between our fellow man, friends, and family is some of the greatest bonds we can ever have. We strive hard to maintain these relationships because of the love and peace that is maintained and worthwhile among friends and family.

Nevertheless, the greatest bond we can have is the bond we secure with our Lord Jesus Christ! Our relationship with the Lord is the most meaningful relationship we can have and maintain in our life. Our relationship must include the giving of thanks to our Lord Jesus, calling on His great name, and telling everyone about the great things He has done. We cannot say enough about the goodness of the Lord throughout our lifetime. It is imperative that we allow others to hear about the greatness of Almighty God in our lives. Our testimony could change the struggle that others are having in their lives and bring them to a place of blessings that brings about great change in their lives and others. As often as I can, I do not hesitate to tell others about the wonderful things the Lord has done in my life. I do not boast or brag on myself but I testify about what the Lord has done, giving glory to His great name. I believe praise is a natural part of the born-again believer's life. When we see all that the Lord is doing, we cannot help but give our Lord Jesus Christ the honor and praise for the great and mighty things He has done. If you want to be mindful of how to honor our Lord with praise and glory consider what the psalmist has declared through many of the scriptures. Such praise and thanksgiving give every child of God a guideline to honor and give thanks to Almighty God. When we consider these guidelines, we are determined to make them a daily part of our lives. When praise becomes a constant part of our life, we will see the benefits of giving the Lord glory, honor, and thanksgiving each day. Have your considered why the Psalms is the largest book in the Bible? The Psalms has much history but the greater part is praise to Almighty God. Let us consider the following:

(Psalms 105:1-4, NKJV)
Oh, give thanks to the Lord!
Call upon His name;
Make known His deeds among the peoples!
Sing to Him, sing psalms to Him;
Talk of all His wondrous works!
Glory in His holy name;
Let the hearts of those rejoice who seek the Lord!

Seek the Lord and His strength;
Seek His face evermore!

November brings us to a time that autumn is at its peak and many things that represent the fall season are moving into position. Throughout the United States the season of Thanksgiving is in full swing. People are preparing for the holiday season by decorating and cooking in order to entertain guest and enjoy the season with family and friends. So much preparation goes into the last two months of the year. Stores are busy preparing sales for the end of November through December. There is an excitement in the air and much anticipation to celebrate the two holidays. During this time of year people are buying things that represent the fall and winter seasons. Hearts are warm and glad because of the love that is shared among one another. Great dinners are being prepared for Thanksgiving and people are traveling all over the country to see family and loved ones.

Throughout our previous chapters we discussed the ability of people to grow great gardens and have much fruit and vegetables to have an abundance for themselves and enough to share with others. As we enter the late fall and winter months the sharing does not stop. It changes from the produce we have grown to the love that the Lord God has grown in our hearts. Our spiritual lives should change for the best every day we are in Christ Jesus. We move away from those things that cause people to be hurt by the words we speak. Our actions change so we will not hurt others causing them to be withdrawn and afraid to interact with each other. I love this time of the year because it seems to be a great change in the lives of many people. A pleasant change that brings joy and happiness to those we come in contact with may change their lives forever. I believe the Lord allows times like this to be in our lives to restore joy and peace in our homes and community. One of the great things during this time is of giving and sharing what we have with each other. It seems that the of love moves on the hearts of so many to be giving and caring for one another. Have you thought about all these wonderful things happening to our family and friends? I believe the Lord Almighty places His love in our hearts during special time so we may desire this love always.

I believe we can have this blissful communion not only on holidays but every day of our lives. It is called living in Christ. If we want the best material things in the world, we would seek out the best stores to buy what we desire. When we live in Christ and desire to experience great and wonderful things naturally and spiritually, we abide in Christ, doing what He calls for us to do. When I was very young, I wished that these holidays would come every month. There was a change in the atmosphere as the love was shared and good things continued for a period of time. I believe if we abide in Christ Jesus it would be like a glorious holiday. I may sound out of touch or out of bounds with reality. Nevertheless, I have witness wonderful things since I have been born-again in Christ Jesus. I believe as the scripture proclaims; ***"Yet I will rejoice in the Lord, I will joy in the God of my salvation. The Lord God is my strength; He will make my feet like deer's feet, And He will make me walk on my high hills." (Habakkuk 3:18-19, NKJV).*** I also believe that when the Lord God comes into our lives, He brings a joyful change that the world does not understand. When the Holy Spirit fills our hearts, a great change takes place. We no longer act or think as the undegenerated person does. The Lord causes a change to take place in our lives and we find great strength in rejoicing in the God of our salvation. Note the scripture: ***"Do not sorrow, for the joy of the Lord is your strength." (Nehemiah 8:10b, NKJV).*** During this time Nehemiah and others were rebuilding the temple that Nebuchadnezzar and Babylon had destroyed. Other nations had come against Israel as Nehemiah and others began to rebuild the temple. These enemies of Israel tried to intimidate them with words and actions that would discourage them from rebuilding the temple. Nevertheless, they continued with the work that Almighty God had given them to do. How often are we intimidated by others as we do the work that the Lord God has given us to do? We will be challenged by the taunts of the enemy, but I suggest we listen to the voice of the Lord and keep working on what the Lord has given us to do. I believe that our success comes by our determination, courage, and above all listening to the word of the Lord God. These three factors will keep us moving with an abundance of courage and strength to complete the task the Lord has given us. I am a firm believer that joy must be a part of the equation in the work that we do for Almighty God. As it is in the natural, so it is in the spiritual. When we are happy with our God given task, the work is easier and fulfilling. We take pride in our work and joy becomes a part of what we are doing, and we will do the best job we can possibly do that makes others happy as well as ourselves.

During this time of harvest and Thanksgiving great joy is communicated between each other because of the nature of the season. People have a great sense of accomplishment and expectation of this great holiday! The word "Thanksgiving" is mentioned numerous times in the Bible having two important meanings: (1) a public acknowledgment of celebration of divine goodness, and (2) a prayer of expressing gratitude. We express joy when we see the arrival of family and friends from out of town and the consumption of a great feast refreshing our hearts and bodies. These are all very good things for our flesh but what about our spirits and souls? With all the excitement of this national holiday we may soon forget the true meaning of this day and the time leading up to this holiday. We celebrate the divine goodness of God our Father for all His benefits that has been supplied to us. Such great things have been given to us that we are often reminded of the scripture declared:

(Psalms 9:1-2, NKJV)
I will praise You, O Lord, with my whole heart;
I will tell of all Your marvelous works.
I will be glad and rejoice in You;
I will sing praise to Your name, O Most High.

Thanksgiving is not just a time of natural celebrating but a time of spiritual celebrating also. When we look back over our lives and see all the things the Lord has done, we will celebrate the Lord our God with all our hearts and glorify the great things He has done. I believe Thanksgiving is a greater spiritual time than the natural celebration. When we celebrate our spiritual heritage, our natural heritage will be blessed as Almighty God supplies and enhances both the spiritual and natural. I believe it is imperative that we allow the joy of the Lord to strengthen His people with the help needed to see us through our Christian journey. When we feel we can do all things ourselves we may fail and become frustrated because things did not turn out as we desired. However, during this time of disappointment did we think that maybe it was our knowledge and wisdom that we incorporated in the project and not the Lord's? The scriptures clearly declare:

(Proverbs 3:5-6, NKJV)
Trust in the Lord with all your heart,
And lean not on your own understanding;
In all your ways acknowledge Him,
And He shall direct your paths.

It is imperative that the born-again believers put their trust in the Lord. The Lord God has given us His word and His Spirit to communicate with us so we will adhere to His way and be successful. It is imperative as children of God the lines of communication with our Savior remain open and we embrace the ability to be able to make our request known before God. Consider the words of our Lord Jesus: ***"Ask, and it will be given to you; seek, and you will find; knock, and it will be opened to you. For everyone who asks receives, and he who seeks finds, and to him who knocks it will be opened." (Matthew 7:7-8, NKJV).*** Our Lord Jesus Christ spoke the word to His disciples, and it is very clear concerning our privilege to make our request known before God. When a natural father loves his children, he will do whatever he can to provide and make his children happy. Now if a good natural father will do the best for his children, what about our Heavenly Father? There is no limit what our Heavenly Father will do for us. Nevertheless, our good relationship with Him is very important.

Therefore, as we celebrate not only the seasons that have been established on our calendar but every day, we are alive and blessed with all the things our Lord God is willing to give us. Many of the people of Almighty God have come to realize that as long as we remain in the will of Almighty God, we will experience the glory of God in our lives. Many of the Lord's children have come to realize that our unity is very important. One of the major reasons that God brought us together is for us to be together, work together, fight the enemy together, and see God's glory together. We will experience our victory as we work together in the kingdom of God bringing down the kingdom of darkness and not bringing down each other. We may be yet individuals, but we are united together with each other and with Almighty God. We have become an unstoppable force in the earth as long as we maintain our unity in Christ and with each other. We will become a highly blessed and favored people as long as we are unified in the Spirit! The enemy would love to stop us by keeping us from uniting with each other. But as long as we are united together in Christ, we will always be victorious! Therefore, I want you to understand that when you come together to celebrate the season of Thanksgiving, let us come together in unity, leaving separation, division, and anger out of our lives. If our thoughts are on the Lord Jesus Christ, we will not venture into the things that will cause confusion and turmoil during our holiday season or any other time in our lives. If you want to see a greater manifestation of God's blessing, treat your brothers and sisters the same no matter what their social or economic status! Together we can stand against the separation and schisms to form a powerful unity that will evoke positive change and generate the real love of God! Real love will allow you to be kind to everyone, giving when there is a need, and picking up those that may have fallen down. But we must remember the real love that brought us into salvation. It is the real love in Christ Jesus our Lord. It is a love so great that the life of one man, Christ Jesus was crucified on a cross for the sins of the whole world that every person would have the right to come to God and be forgiven of every sin and become a citizen of Heaven. Have you given your life to Jesus Christ? Are you convinced by the word of the Lord and the testimonies of others that the Lord will save and prepare you for entrance into the kingdom of heaven? I am fully persuaded that the Lord is coming back to receive His church and we will forever be with the Lord! Now that will be the real Thanksgiving with unlimited love, joy, peace, and great blessings forever! Get ready for that wonderful day.

❖ ❖ ❖

DECEMBER

The Season of Salvation We Cannot Forget

There is a secular song that declares, *"It's the most wonderful time of the year."* This song expresses the joy and cheerful times that friends and families are experiencing. The excitement in the air is electrifying and it moves on the heart of many people, making it contagious in a great way. I think for most people around the world Christmas is the most celebrated holiday of the year. From one continent to another the joy of Christmas moves on the heart of most individuals bringing joy and peace like never before. People are preparing celebrations with friends and family to be remembered for years to come. Huge feast and decorations are in order to bring excitement to ourselves and others as we celebrate this time of the year. Many may have forgotten the real meaning of Christmas but it is impossible for all of us to forget the real reason for the season.

Since the beginning of time when Adam sinned, there was the need for a Savior. Every person struggled under the penalty of sin. Men and women searched for a way to relieve human beings from this penalty. Nevertheless, there was no cure for this awful judgment that Almighty God afflicted on all mankind through Adam. Throughout time, from ***Genesis*** to the ***Gospels*** and ***Epistles,*** the Lord God spoke of a Savior coming to earth to redeem mankind from their sin. Finally after all the prophetic voices throughout time the only One that could save man from their sin was coming to be the only human sacrifice that could save us. When we understand the power of this great sacrifice we marvel and rejoice because we now have a chance to be redeemed and prepare for the coming of the Lord! Let us consider the following scripture:

> ***(Isiah 9:6-7, NKJV)***
> ***For unto us a Child is born,***
> ***Unto us a Son is given;***
> ***And the government will be upon His shoulder.***
> ***And His name will be called***
> ***Wonderful, Counselor, Mighty God,***
> ***Everlasting Father, Prince of Peace.***
> ***Of the increase of His government and peace***
> ***There will be no end,***
> ***Upon the throne of David and over His kingdom,***
> ***To order it and establish it with judgment and justice***
> ***From that time forward, even forever.***
> ***The zeal of the Lord of hosts will perform this.***

When I read ***Isiah 9:6-7***, my soul is happy and overwhelmed that The Almighty God came down from Heaven, entered into the body of a human being, died on a cross, and yet rose from the dead. Our Savior not only did these great things while on the earth, He ascended into the heavens leaving mankind with a promise that He would send His Holy Spirit to fill the hearts of all who desire to receive Him. Consider the scripture: ***"But as many as received him, to them gave the power to become the sons of God, even to them that believe on his name: Which were born, not of blood, nor of the will of the flesh, nor of the will of man, but of God." (John 1:12-13, NKJV).*** When I consider the words, "the power to become," brings about an excitement that thrills my soul! The power to become sons of God is the greatest gift that we could every receive. We were destined to die because of the sin of Adam. The time we were conceived, sin had its grip on every human being. We were destined to die because of the failure of Adam. But God who is rich in mercy, gave us a way out of death through the birth, death, and resurrection of our Lord Jesus Christ. Wow, thank you Jesus, we were given over to sin and death, but now we have been redeemed by the blood of the Lamb! This season of Christmas is the most wonderful time of the year if we celebrate its real meaning. I enjoy all the good and wholesome things that take place during Christmas. It is a great time and there is so much joy during this time of year.

The birth of our Savior gives us (believers) the right to celebrate and be joyful because of the real reason for the season. All of mankind was dead in trespasses and sin. We had no way of escape. But our Lord Jesus Christ came to earth through virgin birth to redeem mankind from sin and unrighteousness. When we give our life to Jesus a glorious change takes place, and not only are were saved by His power, but we become sons of God. Salvation is a part of our lives and we look forward to entering the kingdom of heaven. I have always rejoiced this time of year more than all the other months. It seems as though everything was special and blissful! People were happy and very joyful. Our celebration was not so much as the world celebrated. If the worldly celebration is the only reason, we celebrate Christmas; when the good food, presents, and parties are over, the celebrating is finished, and we go back to the things we normally do during the other parts of the year. Nevertheless, when we have been born-again in Christ Jesus, we do not forget the salvation that the Lord God has placed in our lives. We rejoice every day with praise and honor to the Lord our God. We live with continuous praise and admiration to the God of our salvation. Since salvation entered into my life, I feel like every day is Christmas and all the other holidays combined. Salvation brought great joy in our life and many souls are joyful because of the salvation that has entered into their lives. I love the song I learned during my youth:

Every Day With Jesus Is Sweeter Than The Day Before

Every day with Jesus
Is sweeter than the day before
Every day with Jesus
I love Him more and more,
Jesus saves and keeps me
And He's the One I'm waiting for;
Every day with Jesus
Is sweetest than the day before

I believe the children of Almighty God attract His attention when we offer praise to Him. The salvation we have received is very beautiful to us and to those that witness our loving character. When we are reminded of the loving nature of the Lord our God, we cannot help but show signs of gratitude and love. Songs and scriptures of praise easily come to mind when we see the glory of God blossom in our lives. Praise and thanksgiving are easy as we witness great things the Lord Almighty continues to do for His people. I believe the child of God is filled with the glory of the Almighty so that we do not have any sad songs to sing. We have the Spirit of the Living God in us and the glory of the Almighty surrounding us. Wow, what an awesome Savior we serve! Therefore, it does not matter what things come our way. We are covered by the Blood of Jesus Christ. We are protected from the enemy's attacks. Let's put our trust in the Lord Almighty. I believe that praise is a sign that we are trusting in the Lord. When praise emulates from our lips it is a reflection of the heart. Our heart rejoices of the things that the Lord God is doing. When we walk in the statures of the Lord the beauty of holiness is evident to those watching us. Our lives in Christs are an open

Bible, showing the love and mercy of Almighty God. Our loving kindness is not shown only during the Christmas season but throughout the year. The Lord God has filled us with His Spirit giving us the reason that our joy continues all year. I love this time of year. Joy fills the air and the love for one another is magnified. I believe our praise and worship is as beautiful or even more than the lights and decorations that grace our homes and businesses. When the authentic praise and worship comes from within, we honor the Lord God and the people surrounding us. We also create an atmosphere of love, giving, and joy that causes many people to remember for many years to come, and some will begin to believe in Christ Jesus as we believe because of the love we show them.

We have often heard the expression through song, *"Joy to the world, the Lord has come."* I believe it is because of the manifestation of Almighty God's love in the birth of our Lord Jesus Christ. Jesus Christ came to save mankind from our sins and allow us to come back to God. The birth of Christ, what a great time for all mankind. No longer would we have to remain in sin and suffer the penalty that was brought on us by the disobedience of Adam. We would no longer have to suffer the punishment of sin because of Adam's disobedience. The birth of our Lord Jesus Christ is worth remembering because if we were delivered from the penalty of sin, we are free and eternal life is in our hearts waiting to embrace us. It is time for us to rejoice and be exceedingly glad for the salvation that was made available through Christ Jesus. Therefore, as we celebrate our song, praise, and thanksgiving it will not be in vain. Our celebration to our Savior who was born to redeem us from sin is the greatest gift that all of mankind could receive. We will continue to rejoice not only on Christmas but throughout the entire year, giving praise, glory, and honor to the one that came to earth as Emmanuel to be with us and save us from our sin.

Let us not forget what was done for us through Christ Jesus

our Lord and what He continues to do building up His word in our lives. There are gifts we receive at Christmas time that last for years and leaves an indelible mark on our life. The beauty and longevity of these gifts leave a never-ending appreciation that someone thought enough of us to grace us with such a wonderful gift. Usually when someone gives a gift of this magnitude there is a matrimonial, or family connection involved. However, the love we received from Almighty God was not because we were so righteous or even good, but while we were sinners Christ gave His life that we might have a right to the tree of life. Therefore, let us take time to remember and celebrate the birth of our Lord Jesus Christ. We have so much to be thankful for as we give praise and honor to the One who came into the world, died on a cross, and rose again that we might have a right to the tree of life! Let us rejoice together and see the glory of Almighty God be upon our life.

CONCLUSION

When we study cultures all over the world, we understand that people find time to celebrate special days and times that are important to them. When we celebrate something, it brings happiness and joy into our lives. We look forward to something good as the changing of seasons and holidays occur in our life. We make special preparation with good food and great times that bring us joy and happiness. These times of celebrations cause us to look forward to great festive times that are filled with joy, rest and peace. The things that fill our lives with joy, we wish to keep them occurring and maybe adding more, so life would be wonderful and an unforgettable great time. When we added Christ Jesus to our celebrations it adds the beauty of contentment and peace to our life! Many times, our holidays we are filled with resentment and anger. Family and friends coming together are not at peace with each other because something may have occurred that has caused anger with each other. I believe when we adhere to the word of the Lord and forgive, great things come to past naturally in our lives and the greatness of God is manifested. Consider this scripture:

> ***(Micah 6:8, NKJV)***
> ***He has shown you, O man, what is good;***
> ***And what does the Lord require of you***
> ***But to do justly,***

To love mercy,
And to walk humbly with your God?

These three mandates, do justly, love mercy, and walk humbly with God are the keys to getting along with human beings and the Lord our God. When we read the word of God and we are determined to honor and obey it, we will see the glory of Almighty God. Every holiday becomes a blessed day when we adhere to God's word by loving our brothers and sisters and treating each other with respect and love. Just think, if we live by the word of the Lord many offenses would be settled and we could return quickly to the love and peaceful times that we cherish. Our times of celebration is meaningful and a great blessing to each of us. When we celebrate and show kindness with each other, love increases in our hearts and we discover that our time together to be worthwhile and meaningful. When love, peace, and joy is at the top of our list we will show others how wonderful the God of our salvation really is. I will continually seek peace and pursue it so that my relationship with my brothers, and sisters, and everyone I meet will be a time when the Lord is manifested in me and eventually in those I meet.

During each season during the year I see our victory as we work together in the kingdom of God, bring down the kingdom of darkness and spreading love to every person we meet. We may be yet individuals, but we are united together with each other and with Almighty God. We have become an unstoppable force in the earth as long as we maintain our unity and abide in Christ Jesus. We will become a highly blessed and favored people as long as we are unified in the Spirit of the living God! When we are determined to show God's love to everyone, remember, the enemy would love to stop us by keeping us from uniting and spreading love with each other. But as long as we are united together in Christ, we will always be victorious! Therefore, I want you to understand that when we come together to celebrate the holidays on our calendar, especially the birth and resurrection of Christ, as I have said before, leave the schism out of the house, leave the separation and segregation out of the house. If you want to see a greater manifestation of God's blessing, treat your brothers and sisters the same no matter what their social, economic, or religious status! Together we can stand against the separation and schisms to form a powerful coalition that will evoke positive change and generate the real love of Almighty God! Real love will allow you to be kind to everyone, giving when there is a need and picking up those that may have fallen down! But we must remember the real love that brought us into salvation never stops reaching out and blessing others. When we give to others, no matter what holiday, we are showing the love of Almighty God and compassion to our fellow man. As some has declared, *"It's the season of giving."* There is much more than just giving material gifs. Think of something that will bring joy and lasting happiness into the lives of others. This is what Christmas is really about! Jesus went to Calvary, shed His blood, died, but rose triumphally as declared, that we may have the right to the tree of life!

Each holiday and the cultivation of crops should remind us of our relationship with Christ Jesus. January brought us a new year with all the hopes and dreams that motivate us to do greater and better in our life. Some may call them resolutions, but I call them commitments to our Lord and Savior Jesus Christ that our spiritual life will become greater and the fleshly life will diminish. February is a time when we express love by sharing gifts and affection to those close to us in our life. But I believe we express love to everyone at all times. The love we share to family and friends just might bring them to Christ. All the other months are significant in our lives showing spiritual meaning that draws us out in the open to do things and meet other people. People are making changes from the previous year to make style changes that express the new season. and many are rushing to make these changes. However, the greatest change we can make is the upward mobility of our spiritual life. Not many people desire for things to remain stagnant. We like most things to be progressive, moving forward creating great changes. Just as we admired our progressive gardens, we should likewise have the mindset to see the spiritual progressions in our life. When summer arrives, another change takes place in our fashions, food, and activities. Likewise, things should take place in our spiritual life. Since the weather is warn during May, June, July, and August, most people are outgoing and making contact with other people. During this time, Christians should not be ashamed to meet new people and introduce them to the love of Christ Jesus. It is a great time of year to be outgoing, meeting new people and introducing them to the real meaning of Jesus Christ. This is a great time of year when people are embracing new things. Why not embrace the love of Almighty God through the word of our Lord Jesus Christ. There is a great source of joy and happiness during the mid and latter months of the year. We used the month of September as a special time to introduce to some and remind others that the Lord Jesus is on His way back to receive His church. We do not know the day or the hour, but we adhere to the promise the Bible has informed us: ***"He who testifies to these things says, "Surely I am coming quickly." Amen. Even so, come, Lord Jesus!" (Revelation 22:20, NKJV).*** The event specified in the scriptures is the greatest event to occur for the church. Let's cherish it with all our heart and live a life pleasing to Almighty God that will allow us to go back with Jesus when He comes. October, November, and December bring the changing of the seasons, multicolored leaves on the trees, and the gathering of the last fruit and vegetables of the gardens. October gives us the end of the gardening season and the last of the ninety-five percent of the harvest. November allows the harvest of the various nuts that we enjoy during Thanksgiving through the rest of the winter. Then there is Christmas. There is a song that declares, *"It's the most wonderful time of the year."*

Happiness during the Christmas season is at its highest peak of the year. People are sharing their love through gifts and visits that is bringing great happiness to each other. When our thoughts are on the birth of Christ Jesus, we invoke love and happiness to ourselves and all those we come in contact with. It is the most wonderful time of the year because we remember the One that was born to save us all from the sins of the world. We have a great need to celebrate because without the birth of Christ there would be no salvation for all mankind. But for the grace of Almighty God we would not have the power of a Savior to deliver us from the sins of the world. Through our Lord Jesus Christ we have the right to the tree of life and no longer suffer from the sin that that has us bound.

I am grateful to Almighty God for the grace that covers us from the sin and unrighteousness that's in the earth. We are a bless people because of the salvation we have received from the Lord. I suggest we take time to remember each holiday during the year by giving the Lord Jesus praise and glory for making our lives joyful and happy throughout the year. From New Year to Christmas we celebrate life, especially our life in Christ Jesus. I admonish everyone be happy in the task and professions that the Lord God has given us. When we do this, we will reap the benefits of love, joy, and peace.

REFERENCES

Whittle, Daniel W (1840 – 1901) There Shall Be Showers of Blessing; Daniel W. Whittle, 1883 *copyright status is* Lyrics: Daniel Webster Whittle (1840-1901), Music: James McGranahan (1840-1907)

Faith, Supplication, Encouragement, Prayer, Scripture: Ezekiel 34:26; Psalm 115:12; Genesis 32:26, Showers of Blessing, James McGranahan, 1883 *copyright status is Public Domain*

Author: R. H. Cornelius (1916), Oh I Want To See Him, Tune: [As I journey through the land, singing as I go] Published in 68 hymnals

Warren, Barry Elliott. (1900). Joy Unspeakable

Warren, Barry Elliott. (1900). I have found His grace is all complete

Lehman, Frederick,(1917) The Love of God is Greater Far

Loveless, Robert Claire, Every Day With Jesus is Sweeter Than The Day Before (Published in 11 Hymnals)

Thanksgiving, Merriam-Webster Dictionary, 2020,

New King James Version (NKJV) Copyright 1979, 1980, 1982, Thomas Nelson, Inc.

The Saints and Angels Song

Printed in the United States
by Baker & Taylor Publisher Services